'Moving beyond the rather tired liberal versus conservative dichotomy that characterises so much contemporary discussion of Menzies this work provides a rich contextual study not only of Menzies, but of generations of Australians whose worldview he reflected and helped shape.'
Ian Tregenza, Macquarie University

'*The Forgotten Menzies* is an important contribution to Australian intellectual history and a timely reminder that contemporary cultural appropriation of historical figures can belie the complexity of political thought and action.'
Margaret Van Heekeren, University of Sydney

The Forgotten Menzies

The World Picture of Australia's Longest-serving Prime Minister

STEPHEN A. CHAVURA
and
GREG MELLEUISH

MELBOURNE
UNIVERSITY
PRESS

MELBOURNE UNIVERSITY PRESS
An imprint of Melbourne University Publishing Limited
Level 1, 715 Swanston Street, Carlton, Victoria 3053, Australia
mup-contact@unimelb.edu.au
www.mup.com.au

First published 2021
Text © Stephen A. Chavura and Gregory Melleuish, 2021
Design and typography © Melbourne University Publishing Limited, 2021

Every attempt has been made to locate the copyright holders for material quoted in this book. Any person or organisation that may have been overlooked or misattributed may contact the publisher.

Text design and typesetting by Adala Group
Cover design by Philip Campbell Design
Printed in China by 1010 Printing International Ltd

A catalogue record for this
book is available from the
National Library of Australia

9780522877687 (hardback)
9780522877694 (ebook)

CONTENTS

To deal adequately with so vast a subject as the disintegration of
Puritanism would require a Gibbon.

Hugh Kingsmill, *After Puritanism*

We are, in the Pauline sense, in bondage to the law and can
emerge from it only by the exercise of personal responsibility.

F.W. Eggleston, *Search for a Social Philosophy*

ACKNOWLEDGEMENTS

The authors wish to thank the following people for reading parts of the manuscript or discussing the contents and improving the argument: Ian Tregenza, Malcolm Prentis, David Bebbington, Geoff Treloar and Stuart Piggin. We are grateful to Nathan Hollier at Melbourne University Publishing for his interest in the book, as well as Louise Stirling and Cathryn Game for skilfully getting the book to press. We also thank the anonymous reviewers for helpful comments on the draft manuscript.

With permission from the publishers, this book draws on parts of the following publications:

Chavura, S.A., 'Culture, utility and critique: The idea of a university in Australia', in *Campus Meltdown: The Deepening Crisis in Australian Universities*, ed. W.O. Coleman, Connor Court, Redland Bay, Qld, 2019, pp. 213–31

—— 'The Christian social thought of Sir Robert Menzies', *Lucas: An Evangelical History Review*, vol. 2, no. 12, pp. 19–46

Chavura, S.A. & G. Melleuish, 'The forgotten Menzies: Cultural puritanism and Australian social thought', *Journal of Religious History*, vol. 44, no. 3, 2020, pp. 356–75

Melleuish, G., 'Why there are history wars', *Dorchester Review*, vol. 2, no. 2, 2012, pp. 60–3

INTRODUCTION

Sir Robert Menzies (1894–1978) was Australia's longest serving Prime Minister. He had two periods of office, from 1939 to 1941 and from 1949 to 1966. As well, he exerted a major influence within the Lyons government from 1934 to 1939 in which he served as Attorney-General. There can be no doubt that Menzies as an individual had a major influence on the development of twentieth-century Australia, overseeing considerable change in the 1950s and in the first half of the 1960s as the country was transformed in a range of ways, from the implementation of a program of mass immigration to the expansion of its secondary industry to an overhaul of its educational institutions to dissolution of many of its links to Britain. At a time of considerable change, Menzies appeared to be a rock of stability, a permanent feature of the political landscape, who could assure the Australian people that in a world of change there was something permanent and stable about life in Australia. He was aided in this by the growing prosperity of the country after 1949, a prosperity that was embraced by Australians, many of whom had experienced two world wars and the Great Depression. It seemed as if Australia was being kept on track by a kindly old uncle.

The traditional, somewhat old-fashioned demeanour that Menzies cultivated led many of his critics—most famously Donald

Horne in *The Lucky Country* (1964)—to view him as some sort of outdated imperial dinosaur who had held Australia back from fulfilling its true national destiny. If he portrayed himself as someone who stood for maintaining what is worthwhile in what we have rather than rushing out to embrace the new and the progressive, this left him open to being dismissed as an enemy of change. For later commentators, it did not matter that the Australian Labor Party of the 1950s and early 1960s was old-fashioned and continued to support the White Australia policy. What did matter, as we have argued elsewhere, is that the Whitlam government managed to reclaim the title for the ALP as being the 'party of progress', the party that was full of energy and dynamism.[1] For Menzies' younger contemporary, the historian Manning Clark, the years of the Menzies government were the years of unleavened bread, and Labor and its ideological allies have been ruthless in perpetuating this politically motivated version of Australian political history. For example, former Labor Prime Minister Paul Keating has on numerous occasions spoken of the 'Menzian torpor' that 'rocked Australia to sleep' in the 1950s and 1960s. Of course, the function of such caricatures of the Menzies years in Labor mythology is supposed to prepare the way for him whose sandals no one is worthy to carry: Gough Whitlam.[2] At the same time, Whitlam could understand himself as the true heir of Menzies, especially in terms of his constitutionalism and his interest in education.[3]

In recent times, the Liberal Party has attempted to reclaim the Menzies heritage and to portray him as the fount of the liberal values of the modern Liberal Party. This has been a welcome antidote to the caricature of Menzies, which has often been projected by their political opponents, but which has also expressed certain confusions of its own. Most famously, in 2017 Liberal Prime Minister Malcolm Turnbull stated that neither Menzies nor the Liberal Party were ever 'conservative'.[4] In his speech Turnbull quoted the line in Menzies' autobiography, *Afternoon Light*, in which Menzies explained why he called his party the 'Liberal Party' (rather than the 'Conservative Party'): 'We took the name "Liberal" because we were determined to be a progressive party, willing to make experiments, in no sense reactionary but believing in the individual, his right and his enterprise and rejecting the socialist panacea.'

Political scientist and columnist Peter Van Onselen defended Turnbull's view, reprinting the Menzies quote above, glossing: 'Take the opportunity to re-read that quote, reminding yourself how often Menzies is incorrectly referred to as a champion of conservatism: "determined to be a progressive party". Not a lot of ambiguity in that.'[5] But no serious reading of Menzies' speeches and writings would support Turnbull's and Van Onselen's analyses. Indeed, it is a pity that neither Turnbull nor Van Onselen seem to have read other sections of the book from which that quote was lifted. For example, in the same book Menzies reflected on his childhood debates with his beloved uncle—John Sampson—who, unlike his young nephew, was a socialist. Looking back from his early seventies, Menzies could say that 'Even then I suppose I was an instinctive Conservative'.[6] This wide dichotomy between liberalism and conservatism that informs the analyses of Turnbull and Van Onselen is terribly anachronistic, a mere projection of a wedge between conservatism and liberalism that has emerged relatively recently in Australian history.

David Kemp is far more informative in saying that Menzies' 'individualist liberalism came rather from his legal theory and his Scottish/Presbyterian background'.[7] Damien Freeman's recent history of conservatism in Australia has surprisingly little by way of any sustained discussion of Menzies' political thought. This is a shame given the centrality of Menzies in the history of modern Australian politics, not to mention the considerable amount of material he left capturing his views on society and politics.[8] As we have argued elsewhere, much Australian political thought was a fusion of liberal and conservative instincts, and Menzies' thought can be so described, albeit with the appropriate qualifications that form the argument of this book.[9]

There is a danger in reading Menzies' wartime speeches, collectively published in *The Forgotten People* (1943), as if they embodied the values and ideas of early twenty-first-century liberalism and/or conservatism. Menzies was a product of a particular time and place, and he needs to be understood in terms of the values and ideas of that time and place. For example, much of his memoirs is dedicated to discussing the British Commonwealth of Nations, and by the late 1960s he was undeniably concerned about the fate of the Commonwealth. In fact, Menzies was a loyal child of the British Empire/Commonwealth; he was simultaneously British and Australian, which is to say that he was British in an Australian way, just as his near contemporary W.K. Hancock wrote about independent British Australians.[10] But then so too were most of the people on the Labor side of politics, including John Curtin and Ben Chifley. Chifley was happy to impose rationing on Australians after World War II because he had an obligation to help those in Britain. 'Is it fair', asked Chifley in 1949, 'that the people of Australia, which is far better off than any European country, should enjoy privileges that are denied to the British people?'[11]

What needs to be recovered is an understanding of Menzies in his own terms rather than as a pawn in a modern ideological war within the party he started. Menzies saw himself less as an ideological warrior than as a defender of a tradition embodying both ideas and a way of doing things that he feared was being killed off by a number of cultural, economic and political developments that he believed would come to characterise the twentieth century. He lived through some of the most terrible years in modern history. If anything, he believed—at least late in life—that the age of ideologies was over. Like a good nineteenth-century liberal, Menzies seems to have associated liberalism with good government, not with an ideology.

What is crucial about Menzies is not only that he was on the political landscape for so long but also that he summed up, in his writings and speeches, a set of beliefs and values that were representative of his age. He was not a profound or agile political or cultural analyst; his thinking was not particularly original, nor did he attempt to be so. Nevertheless, there is a solidity in Menzies' ideas that has its roots in common sense and the accepted principles and ideas of his age. Part of this, no doubt, comes from his training in the law. But it means that Menzies possessed a real gift for formulating ideas in a way that was striking for its simplicity. It was his style that made so much of what he wrote and said memorable; he could inspire.

Sir Robert Menzies' political and social ideas have been described in terms of conservatism, liberalism and even civic republicanism.[12] Although these descriptions of Menzies' thought are plausible to varying degrees, they tend to be anachronistically understood in that they project twenty-first-century understandings of these political ideals onto someone who would find those understandings somewhat puzzling. While Menzies founded a Liberal Party, his purpose was not to fight for 'liberalism' but simply to create a political entity that expressed the political principles of a significant section of the Australian population, which believed in individual effort, reward for hard work, and the family. When Menzies did attempt to describe what he meant by liberalism, his thoughts tended to be discursive and superficial, never exploring liberalism's philosophy in any depth. Menzies left little evidence of an interest in cultivating a deep philosophical understanding of liberalism. To describe Menzies as a conservative is equally problematic because he lived at a time when many of the issues that define a conservative today were non-existent and all sides of politics held to values, such as strong support for the family, which today would be termed 'social conservatism'. In many ways he was far less of a 'social conservative' than Labor leader Arthur Calwell, who denounced the 'permissive society'.[13] As many have recently argued, Menzies may meaningfully be described as a conservative liberal, or vice versa. Yet this takes one only so far in coming to grips with the instincts informing Menzies' social thought.

We do not claim that the terms 'liberal' or 'conservative' cannot be applied to Menzies; far from it. Our concern is how those terms ought to be understood when applied to Menzies. Damien Freeman rightly emphasises the Burkean nature of the conservative and liberal traditions in Australia, but there are other dimensions to these traditions that are important and under-examined.[14] We believe that Menzies' social thought may be explained to a large degree as a projection of a cultural disposition that was broader than either liberalism or conservatism but also furnished Menzies with the principles and instincts that enabled him to fuse the two ways of thinking. We argue that Menzies may most helpfully be described as a cultural puritan who was also touched by the British idealism[15]— itself strongly informed by cultural puritanism—that characterised much Anglophone social thinking—especially in Melbourne— during his most formative years. We discuss the idealist influence on Menzies most fully in relation to his thoughts on education.[16]

Menzies, like most Australians of his generation, absorbed the English idea that practicality is a virtue because it deals with the real world. John Henry Newman once described Hurrell Froude 'as an Englishman to the backbone in his severe adherence to the real and the concrete'.[17] Australia, like England, did not really produce 'intellectuals'. Instead there were individuals who recognised both the importance of ideas and the need to achieve results in the real world.

In *The Forgotten People* Menzies rarely uses the word 'liberty' and mostly when discussing John Stuart Mill, but he does make considerable use of the word 'freedom'. What he means by this term is somewhat unclear. He may simply have appropriated it from Franklin Roosevelt, whose fireside chats (1933–44)[18] and famous 'Four Freedoms' speech (1941)[19] were the inspiration for Menzies' own 1942 speeches discussed in chapter 3. 'Freedom' was a common term of the 1940s; it was used by Labor Prime Minister Ben Chifley and is the title of the 1942 Social Justice Statement by the Australian Catholic bishops.[20] The word 'freedom' is more ambiguous than 'liberty' as it can mean freedom of something as well as freedom from something, for example, freedom of religion and freedom from want. Freedom from want has much more to do with social justice than individual liberty.

How then is Menzies to be understood as a political leader and thinker? One real problem is that most people who write about Menzies do so from a republican–nationalist perspective; they have real problems understanding Menzies' strongly professed regard for both the monarchy and the British Empire. Those writing from this nationalist viewpoint simply see the British Empire/Commonwealth as an impediment to the emergence of an Australian nation. This allows them to relegate Menzies to the dustbin of history as an out-of-date and seemingly irrelevant figure. The origins of this view of Menzies as 'yesterday's man' lie in Donald Horne's *Lucky Country* where both Menzies and Calwell are portrayed in this way. Horne described the Menzies of the 1950s as 'more British than the British', 'expressing dreams of Commonwealth that had something of the flavour of progressive discussion in 1908'.[21] Again, this is to engage in an anachronistic reading of the past. Many of Menzies' 'prejudices' were those held by a large number of people of his age in Australia, including more than a few on the Labor side of politics.[22]

Menzies is best described as an Anglo-Australian, as was the case for many of his generation. As with Sir Keith Hancock, he had two homelands to which he felt loyalty; he was simultaneously British and Australian. He belonged to what can be described as Greater Britain. Until at least World War II it made great sense for Australians to see themselves as part of Greater Britain. James Belich has described how the symbiotic relationship between Britain and its settler dominions operated, with countries like Australia sending both their primary produce and their excess intellectuals to Britain.[23]

Being part of Greater Britain meant being not only part of the sterling area but also part of the wider British cultural area, or what would now be termed the Anglosphere. David Malouf has described the middle-brow culture in which he was brought up in Queensland, which 'with a few local variations' could be found 'in any other part of the English-speaking world, from Christchurch to Toronto'.[24] In other words, Greater Britain shared a common form of what Marshall Hodgson has termed 'cultural patterning',[25] and to understand Menzies it is far more useful to consider the cultural patterns of Greater Britain than to attempt to consider him in terms of supposedly universal political ideologies.

It can be argued that Britain and its various dominions were far more attracted to particularistic political doctrines than either the United States or the other countries of Europe. The United States, like France, had to appeal to universal ideas to justify its departure from the British Empire. In contrast, as we have argued elsewhere,[26] the debates of the Constitutional Conventions—occurring in Menzies' early childhood, we must not forget—held to formulate the Constitution that would unite the Australian colonies were remarkably averse to universal political ideologies. Parkes spoke for most delegates when he said:

I utterly distrust paper constitutions. I, for one, with the world's experience before me, utterly distrust the constitution that is framed in the closet, that is framed with the lamp, or that is framed upon same theory or some mosaic made up of several theories ... If, then, we are to construct a government which is likely to give satisfaction and likely to endure, we ought to take the lamp of experience. Now, the lamp of experience held out clearly to us is held out by England and by no other country.[27]

Run by men of affairs and common law lawyers, the conventions primarily sought to adapt the British Constitution as far as was possible to their circumstances.

It is also worth pointing out that Menzies had appeared as legal counsel in the famous Engineers' Case (1920), which established the principle of legalism as the basis on which the Commonwealth Constitution was to be interpreted. Legalism did not embody any real universal ideological principles. Hence, discussing constitutional interpretation, Menzies states:

I do know that in the determination of our type of problem the High Court has developed politically neutral conceptions of constitutional law; an honourable fact which occasionally brought defeat and anguish to my own Government! I say that, because, being politically neutral, though most of the judges had been appointed by my Government, they threw out incontinently some rather important legislation which we had promoted.[28]

Such a view is consonant with views expressed by Menzies in the 1960s: that the age of ideology was over and that good government went beyond ideology and could be based on expert knowledge. It is possible to argue that Menzies was the heir, perhaps the last true heir in the Australian setting, to the tradition, which was also an ideology, which had once been termed the 'Ancient Constitution' and later became the English Constitution, of the capacity of the English political system both to be based on firm principles and to evolve to meet new circumstances. It is worth pointing out that this legal–political set of ideas functioned as a sort of 'civil religion' in countries of Anglo-Saxon origin. As the legal traditions of the West are largely separate from the religious traditions, unlike Islam, this means that the 'civic religions' of the West are only sometimes 'Christian' in inspiration.

Menzies was a man moulded by the English tradition, both in terms of its common-law tradition and its middle-brow culture. He could not be inducted into its higher culture because he lacked a classical education. In this regard he resembles Alfred Deakin, who does not discuss classical texts in his otherwise wide-ranging correspondence with Walter Murdoch.[29] It is also worth noting that H.V. Evatt, who apparently was very good at mathematics, also preferred philosophy and English to classics as an undergraduate.[30] Menzies stood in considerable awe of Sir Owen Dixon, who was both a classicist and Menzies' superior in matters of law. It is worth pointing out that the common element that unifies classicism and legalism is a concern for the specific meaning of words and the need to be accurate when assigning meaning to a word. Although this aspect of English culture was satirised in the figure of Sir Humphrey Appleby in *Yes, Minister*, it was traditionally a great strength of English culture. Care is to be taken when speaking and writing to ensure that what one says actually means what one intends to say.

Menzies' middle-brow outlook on the world idealised the English as the epitome of a civilised way of life. This was not an uncommon view for an educated Australian of his generation. For example, A.R. Chisholm, born six years before Menzies, believed that the true classical spirit of European civilisation resided in England and France.[32] Such men spent their early years during a time in which British power was at its apogee; it would have been absurd to suggest to them that they would be the last generation of that empire. For such men, their world was defined by an international order that was dominated by the British Empire as the key player which held that order together.[33] But the Australian understanding of that order was less hierarchical than that of the British and was summed up in the word 'commonwealth'.[34] This was much closer to an association of equals, with Britain the older, senior brother, than an empire ruled over by a domineering patriarch.

The Roman Empire was marked by the increasing Romanisation of the empire. When Roman colonies were established within the empire, cities were established using a template that marked them out as Roman. Over time—and it was centuries—Latin replaced the local languages, at least in the West. There was never the required time for this to happen in the British Empire, which was, in world historical terms, not long lived. But, as in the case of Rome, there was nothing unusual for provincials in seeking to follow the cultural ideals of the dominant group. They also had no reason to suspect that the empire might be gone by the time they turned seventy. They grew up in age of peace and prosperity when the world appeared to be in a state of harmony and balance. This was the Edwardian 'Indian summer' when Norman Brookes, whose brother married Alfred Deakin's daughter, twice won Wimbledon and Victor Trumper was the world's greatest batsman.

Menzies was never going to understand his world in purely national terms. As a democrat, he was equally never going to see the British Empire as a hierarchical structure based on authoritarian principles. It was always going to be a commonwealth, a commonwealth that exerted a strong moral influence on the world for the better. It was a model of international order. Menzies' world picture was largely built on this faith in the superiority of English values as embodied in the sort of peaceful and moral international order that the Commonwealth represented. He was not, in any narrow sense, a nationalist. This appreciation of Australia as a member of a wider world, combined with a desire for a peaceful, cooperative international order, is quite common among the educated elite of Menzies' generation. It can be found, for example, in the writings of public intellectuals like Frederic Eggleston and Bishop Burgmann as well as H.V. (Doc) Evatt. It fits with the philosophical idealism that they imbibed as young men, discussed in chapter 1. Billy Hughes, a generation older and heavily influenced by Herbert Spencer, and whose approach to the world was tough and realist, stands in stark contrast.[35] The fact that W.K. Hancock's major piece of historical writing was a biography of Jan Smuts, politician, philosopher (and racist) who espoused the ideal of holism (and racial segregation), is sometimes overlooked. Smuts was acknowledged as an influence on Eggleston's magnum opus, *Search for a Social Philosophy*. The idea of an integrated holistic world certainly suited exponents of a commonwealth understood as an association of free entities.

Now, it can be argued that such a vision was an illusion created by the educated classes to justify themselves, and it was exactly the sort of illusion that Glasgow-born philosopher John Anderson spent much of his career attempting to dispel. But it was also an expression of a certain nobility of spirit that impelled its advocates to seek a better and more moral world. It is only once its hold on our minds has vanished that we can see it as an illusion and dissect its flaws. The idealism, the holism, the understanding of empire as commonwealth combine to form a whole; a whole within which the puritan personality—what Menzies would call 'spirit' and the 'independent man'—is its model as summed up in the holistic idea of Personality:

Human personality takes up into itself all that has gone
before in the cosmic evolution of Holism.[36]

Personality enables the man to live his life; it is a battery of
powers, ideas, faculties, emotions, attractions and repulsions
trained and attuned into a consistent and useful whole.[37]

Progress should lead to the creation of a unified whole, both
in terms of society and of the individual. As Eggleston powerfully
argues, the problem with Nazism is that it constitutes a regression
to a lower form of human existence. The issue is how to ensure
that genuine progress is made, by the individual, by society and by
humanity as a whole. According to this vision, Australia is to be
understood as a cooperative entity that, in turn, is part of a larger
cooperative entity, all of which can be understood in terms of the
creation of an holistic world.

Greater Britain can be, and was, understood in a number of
ways, and one of these is as an expression of its Protestant identity. Recent histories of the decline of Protestant England shed
even more light on a tradition out of which Menzies himself
emerged: cultural puritanism. Furthermore, cultural puritanism
was philosophically expressed via the idealist movement in philosophy, which had such a huge influence in Melbourne during
Menzies' most formative years. Alfred Deakin, Prime Minister
in 1908, attended a lecture by Henry Jones when he visited
Melbourne.[38] Indeed, Menzies' thought and language frequently
express the ideals and concepts characteristic of cultural puritanism and philosophical idealism.

The following study describes both cultural puritanism and
British idealism and shows that, during Menzies' most formative
years, these traditions were at the height of their cultural power in
the Australian province of Greater Britain. The book then goes on
to examine Menzies' thought and language in the context of these

intellectual traditions, first by a study of Menzies' famous 1942 'Forgotten People' speeches, then by looking at his subsequent social ideas more generally. On our interpretation of Menzies, an appreciation of the nature and influence of cultural puritanism and idealism shows Menzies' thought and career to be a valiant, albeit failed, attempt not so much to restore liberalism or conservatism to Australian society in an age of rapid social change as to reinvigorate the virtues of cultural puritanism, a tradition of which Menzies was Australia's last great exemplar and defender.

Summary of the chapters

Chapter 1 introduces the concept of cultural puritanism, which, we argue, along with idealism, is the best conceptual lens through which to view Menzies' ideas. This 'puritanism' is not a term made up by the present authors but is a term used to denote a particular culture of Britishness that flourished in the eighteenth and nineteenth centuries and well into the twentieth century, notwithstanding constant lamenting of its imminent death. This chapter shows how the tropes constitutive of cultural puritanism—sturdiness, independence, freedom, self-scrutiny, Godliness, duty, domesticity—were common in the Australia of Menzies' most formative years, setting the scene for the discussion in chapter 3 of his great cultural puritan manifesto: 'The Forgotten People'. Of course there are religious connotations in the term 'puritan', not the least because the term itself derives from the great Puritan movements of the Elizabethan period and, later, those who fled Europe to begin their own societies in America. This is not the small-P puritanism of which we speak. We speak of an echo of or shadow cast by these movements within wider secular culture.

Chapter 2 describes the philosophical idealism that was so prominent in the late nineteenth and early twentieth centuries in Australia (not to mention Great Britain and America). Much has been written in recent years on the idealist movement in Australia, and this literature sheds light on Menzies' intellectual influences. Much of the language and spirit of idealism infused Menzies' thought, particularly his many writings and speeches on education. Certainly the Melbourne University intellectual milieu was steeped in idealism when Menzies was a student during World War I. In particular, Menzies' rejection of so-called utilitarian man in preference for the man of 'spirit'. Although Menzies spoke more of 'spirit' than he did of 'personality', his 'spirit' was essentially the same as the 'personality' of idealists.[39]

Chapter 3 offers a close reading of Menzies' famous 'Forgotten People' speech, first delivered in 1942. We show that this speech, as well as many of the others delivered during this radio series, is an iteration of the cultural puritanism that suffused British culture even up to World War II. In this respect we argue that, although trying to find liberalism and conservatism in his early speeches is not wholly misguided or doomed to be a fruitless exercise, the kind of liberalism and conservatism that Menzies embodied was one that will not be found in modern textbooks of political philosophy. It was the expression of a particular tradition, not captured by Mill, although with much overlap with Burke—himself a 'conservative' Whig. If the 'Forgotten People' speeches can be said to constitute Menzies' mature social philosophy—and he seems to have thought that they did—then there is much to be said for the notion that what he was actually trying to do was to persuade Australians to reconsider the cultural puritan virtues, which he, among others around the world, feared were imperilled by the false promises of socialism and the temptations of materialism and prosperity.

Chapter 4 examines Menzies' wider social thought throughout the 1950s and 1960s, again showing how his basic philosophy was really an expression of cultural puritan values, often with an idealist vocabulary. Indeed, cultural puritanism and idealism were common approaches to discussing social problems around the Anglophone world in the 1950s especially, mainly as a foil against the perceived hyper utilitarianism and technologism of the age. Menzies' social thought lacked any originality, but it was one of the great expressions of a particular kind of theorising—if it can be called theorising—that prevailed especially in the second third of the twentieth century. Unless this is understood, simple characterisations of his ideas as conservative, liberal or liberal conservative fail to capture the cultural depth of the tradition upon which he was drawing and which he was defending.

Chapter 5 looks at the policy area of what Menzies considered to be his greatest achievement while in office: education, tertiary education in particular. It is in Menzies' extensive writings on education that we see the influence of philosophical idealism most clearly, as he shared the concerns of idealists regarding the corrosive effects of utilitarianism and materialism on modern culture and offering the university as the institution best placed to preserve human 'spirit', or what idealists would call 'personality'. Menzies' vision for the universities was that they would produce philosopher public servants, statesmen and experts, if not philosopher kings. Certainly Menzies thought part of the preservation of his conception of civilisation was to be found in an educated aristocracy of government-policy elites—a common idea in the first half of the twentieth century. Menzies' vision of education and the university was a dimension of his conception of a flourishing democracy.

We conclude that Menzies' thought and career are best understood as expressions of a particular strand of British culture described by historians and social commentators since the late nineteenth century as puritanism. This was no fringe movement, and it was capacious enough to permeate both right and left sides of politics. It does seem, however, to have lent itself more easily to the politics of liberalism. We also contend that the language used by Menzies reveals the philosophic idealism that was so influential in Australia throughout the later years of the nineteenth century and strongly during his intellectual formative years in World War I and subsequent decades up to World War II. Philosophical idealism was strongest in the Melbourne of Menzies' university years and early legal and political career.

In a real sense, then, neither the right nor left factions of the Liberal Party entirely embody the ideals that animated Menzies, although the centre-left and left libertarians in the party are most obviously out of step with Menzies' world picture. Of course, attempts by either side to claim to represent the spirit of Menzies are doomed to futility; and why would a modern political party brag about embodying the ideals of a man born during the time of Queen Victoria, who was formed by and responded to social conditions that were radically different from those of today?

It is not so much that Menzies cannot be described as a conservative or a liberal or, better, a conservative liberal. It is that the substance of Menzies' conservative liberalism will not be found in a textbook of political ideologies. It is to be found in a deep reading of the cultural puritanism and philosophical idealism that produced Menzies, and ideals of which he spent his career trying to invigorate in the Australian nation in the face of winds of change brought on by technology and economic prosperity.

1

CULTURAL PURITANISM
IN YOUNG MENZIES' AUSTRALIA

He was industrious, he was honest, he was honorable; his
character was as sterling as his coin. He strove to maintain in
conditions more modern the spirit of the Puritans; he invested
the latter's sincerity with a fuller measure of social grace. And the
admixture still survives in the best type of English character.
'The English race', *Age*, 18 April 1931

'Puritan Britain', in its modern sense, was largely a phenomenon of
the eighteenth and nineteenth centuries; its strongest hold on British
culture stretched up to World War I, but it was still being noticed by
contemporary cultural commentators nearly a generation beyond.
It is no longer with us. In terms of its influence on national policy,
it had a final and, in many ways, spectacular efflorescence with
Margaret Thatcher, who had a strong Methodist upbringing. Its last
living embodiment is Queen Elizabeth II.

Cultural puritanism was an outgrowth of the powerful connection between Protestantism and political liberty in British culture,
which has been described by Linda Colley.[1] This Protestantism
was strongly connected to the political ideals of liberalism,

especially in the form of Gladstonian liberalism. It was no accident that the Australian colonies became uniformly liberal in the second half of the nineteenth century; their political cultures were liberal, Protestant and empire focused. This liberalism expressed itself in such policies as the institution of a 'secular' state education system, which was at the same time very much a project of cultural Protestantism, as Catholics at the time felt.[2] There would be no state church or institutional aristocracy. Even an apparent opponent of liberalism, or at least economic liberalism, such as David Syme was motivated by a strong moral sense, which had its ultimate roots in Scottish Calvinism.

The connection between Protestantism and liberalism was strong in colonial Australia, with many social reformers being of the evangelical type.[3] This can be seen in two of the great protagonists of New South Wales politics in the 1860s: the editor of the *Sydney Morning Herald*, the Rev. John West and arch democrat the Rev. John Dunmore Lang. West was the more conservative of the two, really a liberal conservative, and was critical of the workings of responsible government.[4] Lang was more radical, a fervent defender of democracy. They clashed even to the extent of legal proceedings, but there can be no doubt that both men were liberals and that their liberalism was rooted in their Protestantism.[5] They both supported an independence of spirit; which in Lang's case was projected onto Australia as a whole, as he was a staunch republican. Likewise, if Henry Parkes' liberalism was not, like West's and Lang's, integrated into a theological system, at least negatively he was well known for his anti-Catholicism, which was central to cultural Protestantism throughout the nineteenth century.[6]

Cultural puritanism was characterised by a moral self-confidence borne along by the powerful cultural impact of eighteenth- and nineteenth-century evangelicalism and the buoying effect of the spread of the British Empire. It may be understood as a subspecies of cultural Protestantism, the latter emphasising anti-Catholicism and Enlightenment, not to mention individualism. Cultural puritanism's ethic was a disciplined, world-embracing sense of duty to improve society, but not at the cost of self-reliance and striving, undergirded by a vague Protestantism without the enthusiasm characterising evangelicalism. Admittedly these categories—Protestantism, puritanism and evangelicalism—are highly porous yet each describes certain historical figures better than others, with Menzies fitting well into the puritan and Protestant classes but not at all within the evangelical class.[7] It was duties, not rights, that generated proper moral order, and citizenship was understood accordingly.

Consider the following quote from a speech by Hercules Robinson, governor of New South Wales in the 1870s:

> With complete constitutional liberty, the responsibilities of citizenship are brought home to us all. Every man in this colony in every rank of life owes duties to the community of which he is a member. He has an interest and a voice in public affairs and it is of the utmost importance that his reasoning should be logical and his judgment sound on all matters of public concern … [M]oderation in success, self-denial in the exercise of power, habitual consideration for the opinions and the feelings of others, reluctance to push principles to extremes, readiness to compromise differences, love of justice and fair play, the moral courage which will dare to stand up against a majority, the habit of constantly and as it were instinctively, postponing self to the public interest; these … are the balancing qualities which prevent the misuse of political freedom.[8]

Puritanism, like cultural Protestantism in general, was compatible with liberalism; indeed, the two were deeply morally related; yet puritanism tended to stress independence rather than the expressive individualism of much classical liberalism, particularly as it evolved from the thought of J.S. Mill. The notion of independence referred not only to the character or virtue of the independent person—unlike classical individualism—but also to the fact that such a person is no burden on others. Such a notion of independence was strongly connected to the idea that one should not be dependent on others, especially those who might pretend to be their social superiors. It is therefore no surprise that there is a strong historic connection between ecclesiastical Puritan movements from the sixteenth century onwards and republican movements in England and America.[9]

John Hirst notes the major feature of nineteenth-century democracy in Australia was less political egalitarianism than it was social egalitarianism.[10] Despite the eagerness of many democrats, including Henry Parkes, to be knighted, nevertheless, the notion that 'Jack is as good as his master' remained strong in colonial Australian society. It is captured in the ideal of the 'natural aristocrat', whereby even the child of a convict could aspire to cultivate gentlemanly characteristics.

Independence, or lack of dependence, is captured in the English nineteenth-century liberal theorist Henry Maine, who argued that liberalism involved a transition from status to contract, or the replacement of a feudal-style society based on status to a society founded on liberalism and the individual. However, the British in Australia did not picture themselves as a collection of individuals who were bound together by contractual arrangements. This was despite the fact that the colonies were composed of individuals who had few organic links to their fellows. Rather, they inherited a set of traditional beliefs that particularly emphasised the need to possess property if one was to escape dependency. This is why the crucial legislation enacted after the establishment of universal manhood suffrage in New South Wales was a Land Act designed to turn as many of the Australian colonists as possible into landed proprietors. This was one way in which a more organic social order, egalitarian in nature, could be created.

This ideal of independence may be seen to have its origins in the British tradition of republicanism and the connection it made between liberty and property. The Land Acts would enable individuals to have the material basis of independence. There were powerful distributist currents in Australian culture; there was a general desire that property ownership be spread as widely as possible. Both John West and John Dunmore Lang were inspired by this belief, just as, in the twentieth century, Catholic intellectual B.A. Santamaria looked to the creation of an ideal Australia based on independent small-farm owners. Menzies was himself the product of an Australia that still had a large rural population and relied heavily on exports of its primary produce, especially to Britain. The Country Party was a force to be reckoned with, as Menzies discovered to his cost during his first term as Prime Minister. Canberra had a population of under 10 000 when Menzies became a Member of Parliament in 1934 and still had fewer than 100 000 people when he retired as Prime Minister in 1966. It was little more than a large country town.

Independence was also strongly connected to conscience and the belief that an independent individual will be able to determine for himself the proper and moral course of action to be taken. Most colonial Australians identified as being 'liberal', but to be liberal meant acting in an independent fashion and following one's conscience such that one would follow the call of duty. Again, the cultural Protestantism infusing all of this is obvious and it informed much liberal criticism of the Labor Party and its pledge.[11] As discussed earlier, liberalism was understood as being practical in nature and not as a theoretical system; a recipe that could be applied to create a new kind of social order. It should be appreciated that the British colonists in Australia were very much aware of the dangers of individuals simply doing as they pleased. They were concerned to establish families and to create the institutions and associations that were the mark of a civilised community. They wanted to be respectable and respected, members of a British community. They aspired to be gentlemen. Individuals should behave independently, but that did not mean extreme individualism or licence.

Puritanism and the peculiar form of English republicanism, which placed its emphasis on the relationship between land ownership and the wielding of political power, grew up together, indicating at least an elective affinity between the two of them. Owning property enables an individual to act according to one's own conscience, rather than being beholden to others; the 'sturdy yeoman' was a common expression throughout nineteenth-century Britain as a paragon of virtue. It does not mean acting on the basis of one's selfish interests to the detriment of other like-minded individuals. Rather, it implies the freedom to act in concert with other individuals for the public good. The notion of the independent Member of Parliament, who acts according to conscience—Burke's representative—was very strong in New South Wales in the 1850s and 1860s. This was not a rejection of English notions of the independent gentleman; property owners, of whatever origin, could behave as if they were gentlemen. It was an affirmation of the desire of Australian colonists to become gentlemen. This can be seen clearly in the way in which so many of those in the public sphere acquired the term 'Sir' before their names. Sir James Martin, whose father had been a lowly horse trainer, not only became a knight but also was viewed by visiting writers as the very model of a House of Commons gentleman.

The Scotsman John Dunmore Lang had a similar vision of a social order composed of sturdy independent Presbyterian farmers populating a series of self-governing villages across the Australian countryside. American New England would be replicated in the antipodes.[12] Unfortunately, English country gentlemen had somewhat of a reputation for not only being independent but also being fractious, a quality that Lang himself exemplified and which can also be seen in a number of independent colonial politicians from William Forster to Bruce Smith. The idea that independent men of property who consulted their consciences would agree on matters of public concern was somewhat of a chimera; no less chimerical than it had proven to be throughout the history of Protestantism.

Nevertheless, this is not to say that this form of puritanism, along with its republican sibling, did not exert a powerful influence on the developing Australian political culture. One can see it, for example, in the introduction of the secret ballot as a form of activity in which an individual is free to follow one's conscience rather than being unduly influenced by others. 'Manly independence' is very much a puritan ideal, although Henry Parkes emphasised that the newly enfranchised elector should consult his family before casting his vote.[13] The independent elector should not have an external body to dictate to him how to vote. The same is true of the independent member. The same puritan instinct can also be seen in the successful attempt towards the end of the nineteenth century to remove the power of politicians to exercise their rights of patronage and appoint individuals to the Public Service. Again, it was George Reid, a son of the manse, who instituted the Public Service Board in New South Wales.

It should be seen that this puritan ideal of independence placed a great emphasis on the need for independent individuals to cooperate and work together. Individuals should work together to build a better world and to manage their own affairs. Such cooperation was viewed as being far superior to any coercive practices that belonged to a bygone age. This cooperative spirit can be seen in all the voluntary organisations created in colonial Australia, from building societies to friendly societies to the boards that ran local hospitals. In *Dad Rudd, MP* (1940), Dad Rudd proclaims that the only 'society' (by which he means 'high society') of which he is part is the cooperative society. This also shows the close connection between evangelicalism and puritanism, for it is now well established that a good proportion of voluntary and cooperative societies in the colonies were initiatives of evangelicals.[14] As stated above, the first major challenge to this Puritan ideal of independence can be seen in the creation of the 'pledge' by the Labour Party in New South Wales in 1894, which meant that the majority view of the party had the right to dictate the conscience of its individual members. For many, such as future Prime Minister Joseph Cook, it was a step too far and led to him leaving the party.

Unlike liberal individualism, with its emphasis on rights, independence tends to emphasise virtues and duties. Although the term 'puritan' could be used negatively during the nineteenth century,[15] for the most part, 'right up to the 1960s' it was 'a term of approbation that did not usually denote sexual prudishness but, rather, the more positive attributes of independence, adherence to conscience, tolerance, high seriousness and hard work'.[16] As Matthew Grimley documents, this description of English national character was prominent in English national character literature, written by both the English and international observers, up to the 1950s.[17] Hence W.K. Hancock in *Australia* devotes a chapter to 'Independent Australian Britons'. Although Hancock had a clerical father, he does not refer to religion in this book, but one way of reading *Australia* is to view it as a study of the way in which the exuberant social legislation of the early twentieth century had destroyed the puritan values of individual self-reliance.

Edward Shann's book *Bond or Free*—and Hancock acknowledges Shann in his preface—argues a similar point.[18] Hancock argues that this social legislation, inspired by an older sixteenth-century ideal of 'commonwealth', came to grief on the hard rock of human nature. In the process, it undermined the character of Australians because it encouraged perverse outcomes and placed an increased burden on those who received little support from the state, the independent farmers of the Outback. Hancock was later to repudiate this work as being too right wing. There can be little doubt that he was influenced by Tawney in his use of the idea of 'commonwealth'. Nevertheless, it can be argued that *Australia*, which draws on Eggleston as well as Shann, can be read as an account of the decline of cultural puritanism in the Australian national character. This can be seen clearly if it is read in tandem with C.E.W. Bean's *On the Wool Track* (1910), in which Bean extols the virtue of the independent men of the Outback and their capacity to do anything, a quality that Bean ascribes to their British origins. In Hancock's account, the people of the Bush, who retain their individualistic character, are forced to shoulder the burden of carrying the indebted cities.

As we show in chapter 3, J.D. Green's characterisation of puritanism closely resembles the ethic and rhetoric that Menzies would famously immortalise in his 'Forgotten People' radio broadcasts of 1942, as well as countless occasional speeches to all kinds of audiences, from church congregations to political rallies. In Green's analysis, '[P]uritanism's promise assured all believers that God had endowed each man, through his conscience, with a capacity for what Carlyle called "soul-effort", that is, with an ability for righteous striving. Not only extraordinary but also simple men, so armed, could confront the evil of the world and, to a degree anyway, replace it with good.'[19] As we will see, what Carlyle called 'soul effort' Menzies—in the idealist vocabulary of his generation—called 'spirit', and this 'spirit' was available to men and, crucially for Menzies, women of all classes.[20]

As stated above, the 'puritan spirit' was embodied in the extraordinarily active New South Wales politician Sir Henry Parkes.[21] Parkes looked back to the great parliamentary figures of the English Revolution. He strove to be the 'Grand Old Man' of Australian politics, just as Gladstone was the 'Grand Old Man' of English politics. Hence, we have Parkes describing Gladstone in terms that can only be accounted as an expression of cultural puritanism:

> When in the next age the student of history shall look back upon the succession of illustrious statesmen who have made England the freest, the happiest and the most envied of nations, his admiring eyes will rest upon no grander figure than William Ewart Gladstone. (Loud cheers.) He will recount in glowing language the many achievements for the welfare and peaceful glory of England of one who brought to the work of reforming her institutions and improving the condition of her people, the luminous resources of a matchless intellect, the accumulated fruits of a lofty range of culture, the fiery forces of a splendid moral character and the weight and influence of a stainless character an assemblage of great qualities but rarely found in the possession of one man.[22]

Colonials as well as their relatives in the British Isles spoke of 'sturdy Puritanism', which captured the same virtues of seriousness, independence and diligence that Parkes so admired in Gladstone. In the 1890 Melbourne Federation conference, John Macrossan attributed American democrats' distrust of elected representatives to the 'sturdy independence of the old Puritan spirit'. Parkes, earlier on in the debates, referred to the 'hardy old Puritans'.[23] It is interesting to consider that in his well-known study of three of the greatest Victorian liberals—George Higinbotham, David

Syme and Charles Pearson—Stuart Macintyre describes them as embodying a 'secularised Protestant conscience'.[24] This secularised conscience that Macintyre describes throughout his book is essentially the cultural puritanism historians identify as prevalent at the time, even if it was thought by many to be dying. Its emphasis on independence and duty to others lent itself nicely to the uniquely Victorian variety of liberalism that aspired towards a middle ground between the laissez-faire capitalism of classical liberalism so prevalent in New South Wales and the state collectivism espoused by the labour movement, eventually the Labor Party. Indeed, Charles Pearson, a son of the manse, lecturing to his students on the contemporary state of religion, said: 'The basic moral of Puritanism was self-restraint … Reticence in words, abstemiousness in food, physical purity … and enforcement of covenants were among its characteristics.' According to Pearson, puritans carried their ethos into social life, being easily mobilised for a time of war and crisis. Yet, lamented Pearson, things were changing: 'It is hygiene, not purity, that we seek … Self-indulgence [as opposed to self-reliance?] has become a faith.'[25] Pearson saw that an age of rights was replacing an age of duties.

Cultural puritanism was powerful in the culture of Melbourne in which Menzies spent his formative years. It looked not so much to traditional religious sources as to the great literature of the Victorian age and to the 'prophets' who wrote it. Such literature was understood to work on the soul of individuals, as can be seen in the following quote from Melbourne University classicist T.G. Tucker's *Platform Monologues*:

> We also believe that great literature and its zealous study produce most powerful effects, both upon our inner selves and upon the value and happiness of our lives; that they supply us with a rich equipment, both for social action

and social intercourse; that from great literature we derive indefeasible resources, which form glorious company in the midst of poverty and an unfailing refuge from the too frequent harshness of circumstance.[26]

Despite the fact that in *Culture and Anarchy* Matthew Arnold was highly critical of Protestant non-conformity, it can be argued that while culture is defined in terms of 'sweetness and light', it is an expression of an essentially puritan cultural patterning, not only in terms of its high seriousness but also in the effect it is meant to have on conduct.

In this sense, Menzies stands as an heir of not so much Deakinite liberalism in terms of specific policies but of the moral impulse that lay behind it, a puritan impulse such as had inspired figures including Deakin and Henry Bournes Higgins. But, whereas Higgins was inspired by Aeschylus's *Prometheus Bound*, which he translated from the Greek, Menzies found his inspiration in English literature. John Rickard quotes this wonderfully puritan statement from Higgins: 'Give them [men] relief from their materialistic anxiety; give them reasonable certainty that their material needs will be met by honest work and you release infinite stores of human energy for higher efforts for nobler ideals.'[27]

Cultural puritanism was not a political ideology so much as an ideal of personality, of how an individual carried himself—and we are here largely talking about a group of men—in the world. It was a set of virtues thought to embody the best of Britishness. Its preoccupation with personality, even if the word itself was not very important in its discourse, meant that it was easily assimilable with British idealism. Rickard discusses Higgins in terms of the male groups to which he belonged, including his walking groups. Warren Osmond, in his biography of Frederic Eggleston, uses the term 'aristocratic liberalism' to describe the attitude and outlook of Eggleston. As discussed above, 'aristocratic liberalism' can be understood in terms of a particular type of 'cultural patterning'. Certainly, it placed a primacy on individual conscience but not on absolute individual autonomy. Eggleston, like the mid-nineteenth-century University of Sydney Principal John Woolley, argued that the growth of individuality led to a growing sympathy for one's fellow human beings and capacity for cooperative behaviour.[28] For Eggleston, the goal of the evolution of human society was a state in which individuals would be both moral and ethical and, having achieved this state, would be able to bring the good into being.[29]

For many cultural puritans, the creation of a cooperative order was not only national but also international. In *Australia*, Hancock recognised the conflict between the desire for justice and the brute reality of the international order. Justice could truly prevail only if it spread outside the borders of a particular country. This was the attraction of the idea of the British Commonwealth for such individuals as Hancock. He was attracted to the ideal of a cooperative international order that would be guided by the principles of Smuts' philosophy. Moral internationalism was a preoccupation with Australian idealists and those influenced by the movement.[30]

One of the best ways of discerning the nature of cultural puritanism is by considering what it was not. One good example of its antithesis is Alfred Deakin's portrait of George Reid in his *Federal Story*. To a modern reader, Deakin's picture of Reid looks like a caricature; it is illuminating because it describes those characteristics that Deakin despised. Deakin begins by drawing attention to Reid's unattractive physical attributes:

> Even caricature has been unable to travesty his extraordinary appearance, his immense, unwieldy, jelly-like stomach, always threatening to break his waistband, his little legs apparently bowed under its weight to the verge of their

endurance, his thick neck rising behind his ears rounding to his many-folded chin … He walked with a staggering roll like that of a sailor, helping himself as he went by resting on the backs of chairs as if he were reminiscent of some far-off arboreal ancestor.

Having hinted that Reid was like a monkey, Deakin then proceeds to comment on Reid's habit of falling asleep in public, which may well have been narcolepsy or sleep apnoea and for which Reid could not be held responsible any more than Deakin could for his later senility. Deakin describes Reid's supposed inability to control his appetite; he was 'inordinately vain and resolutely selfish, a consummate tactician even more cunning [than Parkes], if anything excelling him in variety and violence of vituperation'.[31] He accuses Reid of sexual improprieties.

Worse, he describes how Reid pandered to the mob; he made his one long appeal to their sympathy and sensibility and, provided he got it, cared nothing for his own consistency or dignity or their comments upon his 'obvious trickiness and insincerity so long as his cleverness captured their support.' Worst of all, Reid was simultaneously common and partisan:

He knew the average man better than he knew himself for he was the average man in every respect except in his amazing platform powers, political astuteness and the intensity of his determination to carve out and keep for himself in New South Wales and in Australia if possible—but in New South Wales at all events until sure of the other by any means and at any cost.[32]

Deakin's unflattering portrait paints Reid as lacking in higher and noble feelings. Reid is the captive of his appetites and his particular interests. Reid is not 'one of us', and this disdainful attitude is extended to include Reid's sometime lieutenant Joseph Carruthers. Deakin never seems to have appreciated that Reid had to be a canny politician if he was to ensure that New South Wales endorsed federation, especially as there was strong opposition to federation in Sydney.

Oddly, Bernhard Wise is described much more warmly, even though he is accused of sexual improprieties along with Reid, despite Wise's reputation for being duplicitous. Deakin's description of the English intellectual and Gladstone biographer is different: '[T]he Puritan by temperament and training who began as an aggressive atheist and though not a Comtist or formalist in any sense, never consciously outgrew the religion of Humanity, though his intuitions flowered through his grim and gloomy philosophy into a high ethical purity ...'[33]

The real issue is that for Deakin, as for other cultural puritans, 'personality', as idealists used the term, mattered and was central to their vision of liberalism. They desired to be statesmen, not just grubby politicians. The same is true of Robert Menzies, and this can be seen clearly in the memoirs he wrote after retiring from politics.

This ideal of personality can also be seen clearly in Walter Murdoch's summing up of Deakin's personality:

> We may criticize his statecraft, we may find fault with his parliamentary tactics, we may dislike his fiscal policy, at this point and at that we may question the soundness of his judgment; but nowhere will any critic be able to find a stain upon his personal honour. He fought for clean government; and he kept his hands absolutely unsullied. During his long tenure of office, he never for a moment used his power for private ends ... in all his dealings, with friend and foe, he was the soul of honour. Surely it will make no small

difference to the public life of Australia in the future, that in those critical early years when the national traditions were in the making, the most prominent Australian politician was a man who brought into the dust and grime of politics such a clear-shining ideal of knightly conduct ... it was a fortunate day for Australia when Deakin entered politics, with his high ideals, his swift intelligence, his far sight, his boundless energy, his conquering eloquence, all united in an ardent and selfless devotion to the common weal. And his country, in proportion as she is worthy of having had such a servant, will hold his memory dear.[34]

The contrast between Reid as described by Deakin and Deakin as portrayed by Murdoch could not be starker. They stand as emblems of what cultural puritanism was meant to, be and its antithesis. The conflict in ideas is less important than the perceived differences in personality and behaviour. Deakinite liberalism can thus be characterised as the embodiment of a particular disposition and attitude, 'aristocratic liberalism', rather than as a set of specific liberal policies to be adhered to in a dogmatic fashion.

Puritan politics could take a number of forms in the Australian setting. At one extreme there were the various attempts to limit the excesses of the ordinary Australian, especially in the area of the consumption of alcohol but also in such pastimes as gambling. These activities reached their height in the first decade of the twentieth century, with such things as local option. The desire to restrict gambling and drinking was not necessarily motivated by a kill-joy outlook on life. Certainly many, enthusiasts and non-enthusiasts, considered it enlightened and progressive. It can also be considered as part of an attempt, congruent with aspects of liberalism, to enable individuals to pursue a path, not necessarily to perfection, but towards a way of life that would be both more moral and more spiritual. This found expression in Deakin's spiritualism, in the gnostic explorations of Christopher Brennan and in the attraction of theosophy for a small but significant number of educated people. As Higgins put it, what mattered for such individuals was the pursuit of 'nobler ideals'. This is why the puritanism of the long nineteenth century took an idealist turn; material improvement was but the foundation for moral and spiritual improvement. Human beings attained their true nature through the cultivation of their spiritual qualities.

At the other extreme were those political figures who might not have been conventionally religious in terms of their practices but who nonetheless exhibited strong puritan character traits. The importance of this puritan aspect of the emerging Australian culture of the early twentieth century has long been downplayed owing to a focus by many historians on the rise of the Labor Party, the *Bulletin* and such things as larrikinism. The point is that the reason the *Bulletin* spent so much time opposing wowserism was because it was so pervasive. The same could be said of bohemians such as Norman Lindsay who also attacked conventional values.

It was most certainly the case that there was a Jansenist form of puritanism associated with Catholicism, but it is quite properly to be distinguished from what is best described as English liberal/imperial puritanism. It is, as discussed above, the combination of liberalism, Britishness and puritanism that defines this particular group. This is confirmed by the absence of Catholics in the various non-Labor parties, which, as Judith Brett rightly argues, has more to do with culture and values than with class.[35] British identity is a complex entity and has evolved and mutated over time. New elements were added and older ones discarded as times changed. Moreover, 'Britishness' came to mean something different in Australia from what it meant in England. The Australian colonies lacked any real 'Tory' cultural elements and not much in the way of aristocratic culture. Hence the liberal strain of Britishness, as discussed above, was dominant.

Menzies' cultural puritan milieu

Needless to say, Menzies' upbringing in an evangelical Presbyterian household whose head was a small business owner did the most to instil puritan virtues deep within Menzies' psyche. Yet this domestic puritan baptism was reinforced by the presence of a pronounced appreciation for the puritan character evident in wider, 'secular' culture. Victorian schoolbooks were saturated with what we may call cultural puritanism. They stressed duties, godliness, energy, hard work, Britain, nation, domesticity and sturdiness:[36] all the virtues and ideals that would animate Menzies' speeches. Take for example this excerpt from an 1899 *School Paper*:

> The Schoolboy who shirks his lessons may think he is doing a clever thing; but his father and mother and teacher know better. The lesson may be irksome and may need an amount of work that causes weariness and a strong desire to throw them aside; but they are necessary—very necessary—to any real success in life. A noble man was never made by softness and sloth. Everything that is worth having has to be struggled for.[37]

The 'sturdy Puritan' was a common trope in the mainstream Victorian newspapers. As long as Australians saw themselves as predominantly British, the same reflections on national identity circulating Britain, with their stress on cultural puritanism, could be repeated nearly word for word in Australia. Thus Menzies' childhood was still an age in which the *Argus*, one of Victoria's highest-selling newspapers, could publish a panegyric to the sixteenth-century Reformer John Knox, declaring him to be 'an influence as living today as he was in his own age'.[38] Puritan sturdiness and independence was also a trope frequently encountered. In an article on the reception of prohibition in the United States, the same newspaper could affirm: 'The people [of Maine] are mainly of the old English Puritan stock and are consequently noted for their perseverance and general force of character.'[39] Also, still strong was the opinion that the strength and virtue of the American republic was largely owing to its Puritan heritage. The sociological analysis of J.D. Lang was still strong in 1914 in an article on the importance of character in national immigration policy:

> But to the new lands in which the emigrant is casting his lot, to the young communities whom he is joining in the work of building up a nation and of moulding a civilisation, the physical condition and moral character of the emigrant; his education, social habits and general fitness as the stock of a new generation, become matters of great national concern. The first settlers on American soil were Puritans, who sought in the untrodden spaces of the new world the religious freedom denied them in their homeland. The spirit of that Puritan stock still exercises a dominating influence upon the national life of the Republic, is still discernible in its literature and shows itself even in its politics, where the Puritan ideal still guides the people in its choice of the man who, as president, shall rule the destinies of the Republic.[40]

Upon the United States entering World War I the *Age* could trace that country's strength back to the Puritans and their 'sturdy independence and love of liberty'. Furthermore, 'The men of the Mayflower are gone, but their sturdy independence and love of liberty live on as long as the star-spangled banner waves.'[41] Domesticity as central to puritan virtue was also espoused by Australian ministers, whose sermons were published in newspapers on a weekly basis. Thus, the *Argus* reported that one particular preacher 'was certain that a great London newspaper was wrong in stating "the Puritan spirit is dead"'. England was still the strongest nation in the world and 'its strength was in its beautiful home life, based upon Puritan principles'.[42] It is telling that there were already eulogies to cultural puritanism by the 1920s, which, although exaggerated, did indicate the decline of what was frequently called 'Christian Britain'—more properly 'Protestant Britain'. Yet such eulogies also functioned to rouse the defenders of puritan Britishness to espouse these values all the more. Still, by the 1930s the *Age*, in an article entitled 'The English Race', could describe the 'English' in entirely puritan terms, terms that Menzies would almost repeat word for word just over ten years later in his 'Forgotten People' radio broadcasts:

His quiet but conscious sense of self-reliance accounts for his sturdy spririt of independence, a spirit which has roused him to defy and to defeat all attempts at tyranny whether the form was regal or ecclesiastical. For centuries the vertebra of the English nation was to be found in England's sober-minded middle classes. They were men of practical abilities and of humanitarian instincts. The socially ameliorative tendency which characterises so much of the legislation passed in the reign of Queen Victoria bears witness to the fact that if throughout that period the typical Englishman's moral code was rigid his heart was entirely kind. If he carefully studied his trade statistics he was not forgetful of the Tables of Stone. He was industrious, he was honest, he was honourable; his character was as sterling as his coin. He strove to maintain in conditions more modern the spirit of the Puritans; he invested the latter's sincerity with a fuller measure of social grace. And the admixture still survives in the best type of English character.[43]

Such language was employed in W.K. Hancock's widely read *Australia*, first published in 1930. Hancock was at Melbourne University with Menzies during World War I.[44] Hancock, no doubt to Menzies' satisfaction, included the Scotch clergyman J.D. Lang among his four great personalities that shaped Australia. Lang, according to Hancock, sought to populate the continent with 'independent self-respecting mechanics and, still more, of sturdy farmers'.[45] Describing the wave of British immigration from the 1850s, Hancock wrote: '[T]he new settlers were predominantly vigorous, independent, law-abiding Britishers who (to the intense satisfaction of Dr Lang) struggled for decent comfort when they were disappointed of riches, derided the colonial gentry, demanded democracy and observed the Sabbath "with order and decorum".'[46] In other words, puritan Britons, as described by contemporary social commentators. The language of 'sturdy independence' frequently spilled out to colour secular heroes of the empire such as the early modern English merchants, 'who founded the great chartered companies ... [and who] pegged on the claims of the nation in a spirit of sturdy independence which must be an inspiration to all'.[47]

Finally, it was not uncommon to trace the virtues of modern liberal democracy back to the Puritan movement and to view social progress in terms of puritan values—education especially—as working themselves out in a modern world. The Menzies family would have appreciated a 1933 *Argus* article on 'The Power of Presbyterianism', a religion that Robert Menzies never lost an opportunity to identitify with:[48] 'The issues which run like scarlet threads through the religious struggles of Presbyterianism are still lively, even if they be no longer dominant in national life to-day. The principles of personal liberty, independence and tolerance, for which lives, fortunes and untiring effort were spent gladly, are still the great fundamental issues upon which rest the destinies of nations.'

Modern political crises are just secularised instances of the crises faced by the Puritans in the ecclesiastical sphere:

> Presbyterianism expresses in religious terms an aspiration which is intimately allied to the spirit of democracy in political affairs ... The resistance to theocracy and institutionalism which lies at the base of Presbyterianism, the fervent faith in individual responsibility with which it is imbued as a religion, spilt over into every phase of national life in Europe for two centuries.

Furthermore, intrinsic to the Puritan heritage is an emphasis on education; that is, education for all regardless of class. The following sentiments would have resonated with the proudly Scottish Menzies:

> Upon the Presbyterian basis of religious belief was founded a scale of values which gave true proprtion to the loftier things in life. To it may be traced an emphasis upon education and a readiness to endure sacrifice for its attainment that have been diffused through every British community. The call to learning felt by many a lowly son of Scotland produced a long line of scholars and divines whose succession is devoutly maintained to this day.

Finally:

> The impress left upon Australia by the many thousands of men and women who have passed through Presbyterian

institutions is a factor in the life of the State and Commonwealth the value of which is inestimable. Their ideals of
citizenship, their acceptance of personal responsibilities
to the community in which they were reared, their record
of social service of divers kinds are a monument to principles
which no civilised community can afford to disregard.[49]

As will be shown, this last point not only described Menzies'
own family but also neatly summarised Menzies' own conception of the ideal citizen, as famously described in his 'Forgotten
People' broadcast of 1942. Thus, the puritan ideals of sturdy independence, the sanctity of domesticity, labour and thrift and the
duty-centric foundations of democracy were common cultural
puritan tropes during Menzies' childhood and early career.

2

THE IDEALIST MILIEU

As well as cultural puritanism, Menzies' thought seems to have also imbibed a somewhat more philosophical spirit, that of idealism, which was distinct from but by no means incompatible with the cultural puritanism circulating during his early years. Indeed, the cultural puritanism animating the idealist philosophy of T.H. Green was frequently pointed out by Green's contemporaries and has been demonstrated more recently.[1] The poet Algernon Swinburne complained of the lectures of Green, 'who preached Hegel with the accent of a puritan'.[2] Notwithstanding the practical instinct—frequently and ambiguously described as 'utilitarianism'—constraining much Australian political and social thought, Green's influence on Australian intellectual life was significant in the 1890s. Indeed, as Marian Sawer writes, 'Green's political philosophy may have appealed to Australian reformers because ... his was an eminently practical creed.'[3] For example, Melbourne University's idealist professor Henry Laurie—who taught Walter Murdoch—in his 1897 Moral Philosophy examination included four questions (out of nine) on idealist philosophy, three of them focusing explicitly on Green.[4] As Marnie Hughes-Warrington and Ian Tregenza show, Australian idealism came into prominence in the debates leading up to Federation and remained strong until after World War I and up to World War II in Melbourne, where idealism survived the assaults of materialism and realism that smashed it in Sydney under the influence of the Scottish philosopher John Anderson.[5] In other words, Menzies' most formative years coincided with cultural puritanism and idealism's glory years. Indeed, Menzies developed an intellectual approach and a rhetoric that embodied the puritan tradition described by historians with an idealist inflection.

Idealism, as the word indicates, placed a primacy on ideas or spirit as constituting the true nature of the universe. It looked back to Platonism, but it also viewed the world in dynamic (Hegelian) terms as the realisation of spirit over time. It brought together an historical understanding of the universe with an appreciation that the central forces driving that history were intellectual and spiritual in nature. Importantly, progress was not merely about material improvements in the human condition, including a growing affluence and an amelioration of the conditions under which people lived. Also, progress was not guaranteed merely by advances in science and technology, as many cruder utilitarians and secularists maintained. Progress also meant gains that the human race had made in its moral and spiritual condition, as well as intellectual improvements. Menzies would stress this distinction between material—technological and economic—and moral improvement from his earliest writings in the *Melbourne University Magazine* until the end of his political career. At a local level, the expansion of the British Empire was to be understood as being motivated by the desire to make profits; the British Empire was a device for spreading the light of science and true morality into the darkest corners of the earth. It was the carrier of a genuinely spiritual mission.

Taken in a broad sense, idealism as a philosophy can be viewed as part of a concern of the British world in the nineteenth century to create a culture that was not rationalist and materialist. The movement was, to a large degree, a critique of utilitarianism in its more dogmatic, materialist forms. In this respect the prevalence of idealism in Australian intellectual life and public policy, along with other intellectual traditions,[6] must serve to restrain any claims of Australia as simply a 'Benthamite society'.[7] This desire to give primacy to the spiritual over the material can be seen as running from the Romantic poetry of Wordsworth and Coleridge to the Pre-Raphaelites and the poetry of Tennyson. It manifested itself in a range popular culture interests, including spiritualism. And, in the form of theosophy, it took ideas from one of its dependencies and created a new type of religious philosophy.[8] At the core of idealism was a faith that a new, better and more spiritual world was coming into being, a world that would realise what was best in human nature. True human nature was both spiritual and cooperative; its realisation could even be understood as the bringing into being of God through cultural evolution. In the case of Menzies, this optimism is most obvious in his justification for expanding the university sector (see chapter 5).

Alfred Deakin also exemplifies the connection between cultural puritanism and English idealist philosophy. When the Hegelian philosopher Henry Jones, whose book *Idealism as a Practical Creed* (1909) Deakin read and reread, visited Australia in 1908, Deakin attended at least one of his lectures and had dinner with him.[9] Jones identified his own generation as 'the heirs to the still unexhausted inheritance of the stern virtues of the Puritan Age'.[10] There are positive references to idealism in Deakin's correspondence with Walter Murdoch, and his reading in the area was extensive.[11] Murdoch asserts that Deakin's 'attitude to life was a religious attitude'. It was deeply spiritual even as Deakin made little public avowal of his spiritual concerns. Deakin, of course, was a spiritualist with a deep interest in religion.[12] In a country in which a major magazine like the *Bulletin* mocked religion, public declarations regarding religion might not be a sensible move by a political leader; religion was something best left to the private sphere.

Idealism was attractive to Deakin, who combined spiritual concerns with an abiding concern for moral rectitude. Idealism as a philosophy was essentially aspirational in nature in that it strongly emphasised how individuals should behave and saw the attainment of such behaviour as part of the spiritual evolution of humanity. Realism in Australia, especially as it came to be expressed by John Anderson, was deeply pessimistic, leading Anderson to conclude that history made much more sense as decline than as progressive evolution.[13] Andersonianism effectively killed off idealism in Sydney during the late 1920s and 1930s.[14] It continued somewhat longer in Melbourne, with one of its last expressions being Eggleston's *Search for a Social Philosophy* (1941).

Deakin, of course, lived his lucid life prior to 1914, before the pessimism induced by the horrors of World War I had its effect. The British Empire was challenged but still appeared to be supreme. The British world was perhaps at its apogee. As Hughes-Warrington and Tregenza point out, 'a distinctive Australian form of New Idealism emerged by Australian Federation in 1901', which 'can be distinguished from British idealism by its greater emphasis on "empire", "humanity" and "international order", rather than the "state" as analytical categories'.[15] This empire-centric idealism profoundly informed the Australian—especially the Victorian—intellectual culture in which Menzies was formed. What comes after World War I is the response to its terrible events. One is realism, another is restatement of cultural puritanism in its idealist mode, taking into account the horrors of the age with which a young Menzies attempted to come to grips. Reading Belich, it appears to be the case that the 'British world' became more defensive in the period between the wars, attempts being made to ensure that strong bonds existed between the various 'settler' members of what was becoming the Commonwealth. Menzies is the product of the transition to this new, more pessimistic age; he hangs on to the idealism and cultural puritanism, but the former is no longer the exuberant set of values which it had been for Deakin.

This corresponds with the long-held view that something 'went wrong' with Australian culture as a result of World War I with the extinguishing of a certain optimism, which had only been dented by the Depression of the 1890s. This optimism can be seen in the various handbooks produced for visitors to the British Association for the Advancement of Science Meeting in 1914. Equally, one can taste the new pessimism in V.G. Childe's *How Labour Governs*, written in 1922. Menzies describes the cynicism of Billy Hughes in his memoirs,[16] yet one discovers a youthful optimistic Hughes as he describes the Labour utopianism of the early 1890s.

There may have been a time when all seemed possible and Australia was the 'social laboratory' for the world. Certainly, Deakin's political achievements could be interpreted in this light. But, as has been argued elsewhere, Keith Hancock's *Australia* was a sober reassessment of earlier utopian hopes and how Australians had been mugged by reality. As Depression followed ten years after the 'war to end all wars' so the response was not a desire to exit the British world but to cling ever more closely to it. For intellectuals such as Hancock and Duncan Hall, as well as the Australian idealists, the British Commonwealth came to embody an ideal of—or a possibility of—what the British cultural and political tradition could achieve. It was a representative of an older generation, Billy Hughes, who expressed in a clear and forceful fashion the doctrine of realism in international affairs. Hancock recognised the ubiquity of Machiavelli in the modern world but still held hopes that a world founded on ethical ideals could come into being.

Now, it can be argued that this lingering idealism was essentially the expression of an older vision of the world and how it worked, one that had been stimulated by the great literature of the Victorian age, as well as the idealist philosophy of T.H. Green and his successors. There was an overhang of an earlier age, one perpetuated perhaps by the continuing presence of Victorian literature, especially the poetry, in the school English curriculum.

Idealism and the young Menzies

This was the world that Menzies, like his contemporary in the Labor Party H.V. Evatt, inhabited. He turned twenty in 1914, having spent his teenage years in the Edwardian Indian summer. He had to reconcile the new brutal world of war and its aftermath with the warm glow that idealism and all things British gave him. Exactly the same was true of Keith Hancock. The war had shaken English ideals badly, but it had not come close to destroying them. English puritanism had, in a sense, been strengthened by the war. In the middle of the war, Menzies, now a university student, reflected:

> It is because we consider this war as, above all things, a vindication of truth and justice and liberty as against a system of deception, violence and servitude that we are able to walk around with a clear conscience ... We unhesitatingly admit that in this war, as in most wars, we are to a certain degree fighting for our own existence as an independent state. But above all, we believe in our final victory simply because we believe that, *in all the spiritual forces which alone can bring about a lasting peace, Great Britain has been and is, superior to her enemies.*[17]

It was what had made the British world great; God had not deserted it.

But, as the early 1920s demonstrated, something had changed and the British Empire could no longer simply be taken for granted. There was now a shrill quality to British patriotism as it found expression in the 1920s. This can be seen clearly in the revived sectarianism of those years. The British Protestant nation needed to defend itself against the forces of Catholicism, especially now that the source of that Catholicism, Ireland, was a separate country. Between 1922 and 1925 New South Wales was ruled by a government which had a cabinet that was entirely Protestant in nature. Hence the Englishness that informed Menzies' cultural horizons was much more self-conscious than it had been at the time of the empire's zenith. It could no longer be just assumed. It needed careful exposition. It needed to be defended. And the same was true of English puritanism. If Hancock's *Australia*—and, later, Menzies' 'Forgotten People'—exposed the declining puritan spirit in Australia, then a need existed for Australians to be even more self-consciously British than ever.

Idealism was central for the generation of young men and women who were fortunate enough to attend university between about 1880 and 1914. Menzies stands right at the end of this generation, attending the University of Melbourne during World War I. Idealism was broad in its concerns, analysing not only moral and political concepts but also global affairs.[18] There is also great significance for the present study in British idealism's critique of utilitarianism as an impoverished and dehumanised social philosophy, as well as its critique of classical liberalism's *laissez-faire* economics, the latter critique most famously associated with T.H. Green.[19] Both of these traits of British idealism were strongly present in Menzies' thought, the former in particular manifesting in his thoughts on democracy and education. Indeed, the language of idealism infused the *Melbourne University Magazine*, which Menzies would eventually edit in 1916, not to mention Menzies' own published essays in it.

The idealism of the magazine during Menzies' student years reflected the philosophical inflection of the Melbourne intellectual scene in general. In a pseudonymous article entitled 'Have we any culture?', the writer criticises the utilitarian approach to life, which reduces the valuable to the practical and praises the medieval university as a custodian of culture. The lesson for Menzies' generation was clear:

> A University is all the more necessary in this age of Commercialism, in order to provide something permanent and worth while amid a scene of change and excitement and selfishness, but it seems as if the University is just going to descend to the already sickening level of the life about, instead of remaining something to which the world can look.[20]

The writer went on to criticise students for being more wedded to the sort of appearance befitting their class than being wedded to real education. They are more interested in carousing and reading fashionable novels than educating themselves.

Another pseudonymous writer submitted 'Science and mind', which offered a typically idealist critique of scientism, not unlike that which Menzies would trot out for the whole of his career: 'It seems, unfortunately, that people have been led on by the obvious, not to say, superficial, advancements of science in relation to industry into believing that our highest goal can be reached along the path of materialism.'[21]

In 'Education and truth', Menzies repeated the common idealist critique of 'those baser and more utilitarian conceptions of education', with their emphasis on practicality at the expense of 'the eternal quest for Truth'. On the contrary, 'Education is thus essentially ethical in purpose; it is the cultivation of the highest in man and the negation of all those lower elements which would drag him down.' Anticipating observations he would make throughout his political career, Menzies condemned the philistinism of his age, in which 'we find that so many look on the education of our youth as the acquisition of so many rules and so many formulae—just so many as will enable them to fill some niche in this workaday world'. He went on, 'we somehow fail to see that in this way the true ideal of Education is almost as completely negatived!'[22]

All of this was distilled in Matthew Arnold's widely read *Culture and Anarchy* (1869), which also lumped evangelicalism in with utilitarianism for its rejection of culture and learning for emotionalism. Menzies would similarly react against his own father's religious enthusiasm in favour of a broader Protestantism or cultural and aesthetic Christianity. Although Arnold's target in *Culture and Anarchy* was English nonconformity and its provincial spirit, it can be argued—as did Trevelyan[23]—that Arnold himself possessed a devotion to duty that was essentially puritan in its nature. Arnold was certainly no aesthete devoted to art for art's sake, and in his devotion to the 'best self', which he saw in terms of serving the state, he can be seen as being driven by a powerful puritan instinct. At times Arnold reads as being quite similar to T.H. Green, and both he and Green can be considered authors who brought together puritanism and a broader appreciation of human nature. Philosophical idealism brought together the vocational duty of puritanism with an appreciation of humans as being spiritual beings. Arnold, the Hellene, was a great admirer of the Cambridge Platonist John Smith. The idealism of the late nineteenth century had an elective affinity with the Platonic traditions of English religion as exemplified by Smith and with a 'Broad Church' tradition of the toleration of religious diversity.

In his 1916 article 'The place of the university in the life of the state', Menzies applied the same duty-centric conception of citizenship that would characterise his later public thought to the university:

The University must realise—we must all realise—that our responsibility to the community is a tremendous one. Having received much, we must give much. It is not childish to have ideals; they are the motive force of all purposeful action; and when we begin to have high ideals of what we can do for the State, when we have learned to look beyond the comparatively narrow bounds of our particular profession to a great world crying for light and leading, then and not until then, shall the stigma of separateness be removed from us.[24]

Thus, in Menzies' earliest published writing, his moral concepts and vocabulary strongly mirrored the idealist tradition as it had emerged in Melbourne over the generation before his enrolling in university. Indeed, there were two prime ministers in Australian history who showed strong idealist tendencies in their thought and language: Sir Alfred Deakin and Sir Robert Menzies. Deakin and Menzies were also the first two Australian prime ministers to attend Melbourne University, both during its idealist phase.

As stated above, cultural puritanism and idealism were complementary; each of them in its own unique way emphasising duties over rights and the moral status of the collective as well as the individual. This kind of ethic was prominent in the thought of Scotland-born Australian academic Sir Walter Murdoch, who was heavily influenced by British idealism and whose father was a minister in the Free Presbyterian Church.[25] As has already been noted, Murdoch was the biographer of Alfred Deakin. His little book, *The Australian Citizen: An Elementary Account of Civic Rights and Duties* (1912), was widely read and written as a school textbook. Despite its title, it had nearly nothing to say about civic '*rights*', focusing instead on moral and civic duties and virtues. Thus, for Murdoch, ideal citizens are 'men and women trained to reflect, to reason and to observe; trained also to be masters of themselves, to control their passions, to do their duty'.[26] As Menzies would do thirty years later in his 'Forgotten People' speech, Murdoch described the domestic sphere—'the home'—as central to the production of good citizens; indeed, citizenship was simply domestic morality writ large:

> The virtues of the good citizen are just the plain, everyday virtues we learn in our own homes. And indeed, the home is the great school and training ground of citizenship; in our early days, among our brothers and sisters, we may learn all that is needed to fit us for playing our parts in the larger life of the state. For it is in these days that we are taught the great lessons of love and kindness, of obedience and truthfulness, of courtesy and consideration for others, of respect for what is higher and compassion for what is weaker than ourselves; and it is just on these things that good citizenship is based.[27]

The idealist philosopher F.W. Eggleston, also nourished by the Melbourne intellectual scene (although he did not attend Melbourne University) and a Methodist upbringing, espoused a civic ethic based on independence and the common good. He wrote:

> … further social advance, if it is to be a real advance, involves qualitative as well as quantitative factors, that we cannot advance by developing the mechanical factors only in our system of ideas, that activity, inspired by enlightened purpose based on personal responsibility of the individual, with a disinterested desire to secure the good life for all, is essential if our problems are to be solved.[28]

Eggleston highly prized human cooperation as being a manifestation of the evolution of human beings and saw totalitarianism as a reversion to a more 'primitive' stage of human development. Eggleston acknowledged the influence of the idea of Holism,

developed by the South African politician and philosopher Jan
Smuts, on his thought. He claimed that he was translating Smuts'
approach into the social sphere. W.K. Hancock wrote a two-
volume biography of Smuts and was also clearly influenced by
him. Smuts, claimed Hancock, was the man who coined the term
'British Commonwealth', and there would appear to be a connection between support for the Commonwealth ideal in international
affairs and the ideal of an evolving cooperative world based on
ethical growth.

Certainly, this was the basis of Eggleston's social theory.
Eggleston understood the ideal social order as an outgrowth of
what he termed the 'Christian Ethic'. 'If we were all Christian in
our conduct, social life would also be perfect,' he argued.[29] One
crucial element of that ethic he defined as the 'universal personal
responsibility for right action prompted by right feeling as distinguished from mere obedience to laws and maxims'.[30] Eggleston
was arguing essentially that the goal of human social evolution
was a puritan Christian Commonwealth, but one based not on
religious belief but on Christian culture. It is a fusion of idealist
evolution and puritan ethics but in a world that is not explicitly
Christian in a religious sense. It is also an ethical program that has
a real-world goal. Here is Hancock expounding his vision of the
British Commonwealth: 'It is a programme which grows out of our
own history. The guiding thread in our history is liberty. It gives
the clue to our past achievement, it explains the unity which makes
us strong to-day and the service which we are rendering and shall
render to the welfare, freedom and security of all peoples.'[31]

The Commonwealth can be viewed as the material expression
of a set of values that have their roots in the puritan idealist personality. In the final analysis it was a utopian dream that can be
placed alongside the other utopian dreams of the twentieth century: capitalism, communism and fascism. It was always doomed;

Smuts believed in Holism but practised separate racial development. It can surely be no accident that the death knell of the British Empire coincided with that of puritan idealism.

All of these conceptions of civic agency were a far cry from what some thought really characterised Australians. Just twelve years before Menzies' 'Forgotten People', Hancock had famously described the Australian attitude to the state as 'a vast public utility, whose duty it is to provide the greatest happiness for the greatest number'.[32] Hancock went on: 'Each of these individuals is a citizen, a fragment of the sovereign people; each of them is a subject who claims his rights—the right to work, the right to fair and reasonable condition of living, the right to be happy—from the State and through the State.'[33] Not quite the ideal citizenry as described eighteen years earlier by Murdoch and twelve years later by Menzies. Hancock's characterisation of Australia can be considered as the consequence of the failure of the puritan spirit.

Indeed, as discussed recently by S.J.D. Green in his *Passing of Protestant England*, commentators of the time were lamenting the decline of the puritan spirit. Hancock himself wrote that 'the period of "fair and reasonable", of "independent Australian Britons", is already closed'.[34] Field Marshal Jan Smuts—one of Menzies' contemporaries and heroes—in a St Andrews University address in 1934, lamented, 'The disappearance of the sturdy, independent-minded, freedom-loving individual and his replacement by a servile standardised mass-mentality is the greatest human menace of our time.' Not merely significant for expressing a discourse that Menzies had clearly latched onto, Smuts' words were written down by Menzies for his private contemplation, as was his habit when he came across books and treatises that he considered insightful.[35] He would quote Smuts again to the same effect in a speech delivered in 1935–36: 'The sturdy individualism which inspired progress in the past, which made Rome, which made

Scotland, which has created all our best human values, seems to be decaying in the atmosphere of confusion and disillusion of our day.'[36]

Smuts had fought against the British in the Boer War but had come to appreciate the worth of the British Commonwealth. Smuts, Hancock and Menzies were all from the periphery of the British Empire, from autonomous entities who viewed the empire as a commonwealth of free peoples. They resisted the notion of imperial federation. The Commonwealth was to be founded not on power, as Hancock saw manifested in Machiavellianism, but in the spirit of friendship and cooperation. It was, of course, a dream full of contradictions, but a dream based on noble motives. Certainly the ideal of an international order based to a large extent on friendship and cooperation animated by deep moral ideals was something Menzies espoused until the end of his career as prime minister. Such thinking was powerful globally, finding its institutional expression in the League of Nations.

Menzies had been born into a world of comparative peace in 1894, then lived through the horrors of two world wars as well as the Cold War. Like Hancock, he sought an antidote to the great inhumanity of the first half of the twentieth century in an idealised Britishness/Englishness that contemporary historians like Trevelyan and social commentators called puritanism. As the world descended into madness in the 1930s, such figures found refuge in an idealised model of England as the one place in the world where human decency and civilised values continued to flourish despite the gathering storm. This ideal of England was reinforced by Menzies' visit to England in 1940. In many ways, this idealisation can be found in the 1937 depiction of Hobbiton by the English Catholic writer J.R.R. Tolkien, who was two years older than Menzies.

Read in the light of cultural puritan sentiments and tropes, as well as the profoundly influential movement of philosophical idealism, 'The Forgotten People' and Menzies' social thought in general become less a liberal or conservative manifesto than an apology for the cultural puritanism that many contemporary commentators said characterised the English personality at its best, but which, according to as many commentators, was also fast declining. Indeed, this puritan ethic was highly compatible with liberal and conservative instincts, not to mention the strong tradition of idealism that pervaded Melbourne's intellectual culture during Menzies' most formative years. At the end of the day Menzies' great inspiration was less Burke and Mill considered as political theorists and more a conception of Britishness as viewed and idealised, from the periphery of empire. Sometimes Mill's thought could fit within this structure, sometimes not. Yet, of the two political thinkers, Burke's instincts are far more compatible with Menzies' than those of Mill. This may be because Burke, unlike the rationalist Mill, saw himself as definitively stating and defending what he took to be the legal, political and social instinct that constituted Britishness. In this light Menzies' thought and career may be understood as an attempt to resuscitate an ideal dying at the hands of myriad forces—affluence, social pluralism, Empire decline and secularisation—discussed by subsequent historians and sociologists. It is to his most famous statement of his political and social views that this study now turns.

3

THE *FORGOTTEN PEOPLE* SPEECHES

The best and strongest community is not that in which
everybody looks to his neighbour hoping for something from
him, but that in which everyone looks to his neighbour, willing
and able to do something for him. In brief, we achieve the good
of man when we help and encourage him to be a man—strong,
self-reliant, intelligent, independent, sympathetic and generous.

Menzies, 'The task of democracy'

In this chapter we will attempt to reconstruct a coherent political world view from the document that Menzies claimed to
represent his considered 'political philosophy': his speeches delivered in 1942 and subsequently published as *The Forgotten People
and Other Studies in Democracy*. Rather than being principally
concerned to argue about the liberal or conservative inflection
of the thought animating these speeches, we will show how the
speeches' principal tropes and normative ideals are, for the most
part, an expression of the cultural puritanism that animated much
of British culture. Indeed, shades of what today might be termed
liberalism and conservatism are evident in these speeches, but

these are merely modes of a broader and far more encompassing puritan world picture that Menzies imbibed and spent much of his life trying to defend from puritanism's twin enemies: socialism and radical individualism.

It should be said that these years produced a number of works that sought to address what was perceived to be a 'crisis of civilisation'. Menzies provided an answer to that crisis, which said that the best answer to the challenges of the day was to reassert those values and ways of doing things that had worked in the past and which had made the British people great: personal responsibility, individual exertion and a willingness to do one's duty. Menzies was not opposed to the state or the role that the state needed to play in the life of the people.

In *The Forgotten People* Menzies focused on the meaning of freedom in a democracy. In so doing he provided an exposition of the meaning of freedom that had its roots deep in the sensibility of puritanism. He was not propounding an abstract theory of the individual or liberalism but expounding a set of social values appropriate for Australians at a time of crisis. In 1942, with Australia facing a real existential threat, there was a sense in which an old world had died and a new world was waiting to be born. Menzies was putting the case for the values that he believed had successfully guided the British over an extended period.

These values were nicely captured in G.M. Trevelyan's *English Social History*, first published in 1942, the year 'The Forgotten People' was delivered. His description of the 'Puritan character' is not to be found in his section dealing with the Elizabethans but in his discussion of 'Evangelical influences' in the early to late nineteenth century:

The Victorian gentleman and his family were more religious in their habits and sober in their tone of thought than their predecessors in the light-hearted days of Horace Walpole and Charles Fox. The English of all classes formed in the Nineteenth Century a strongly Protestant nation; most of them were religious and most of them (including the Utilitarians and Agnostics) were 'serious', with that strong preoccupation about morality which is the merit and danger of the Puritan character ... An individualist commercialism and an equally individualist type of religion combined to produce a breed of self-reliant and reliable men, good citizens in many respects ...[1]

Pages later Trevelyan took up the subject again:

The [eighteen] 'seventies and 'eighties had been a period not only of large families but of puritanism in ethical and sexual ideas, qualified by the too frequent weakness of human nature in practice. Queen Victoria had put the example of her court on the side of the stricter code. The genuine honesty of most British merchants as men of business had been one of the causes of our great commercial prosperity. The popular heroes of the period—and they were true heroes—were religious men first and foremost: Livingstone the African explorer and missionary; General Gordon the soldier–philanthropist; Lord Shaftesbury and Mr Gladstone; to these four, so different from one another and from everyone else, life was the service of God ...[2]

Independence rather than individualism was the central virtue for Menzies, and it occurred frequently in his *Forgotten People* speeches. Independence almost constituted Menzies' civic religion, and he frequently invoked it using religious language and allusions. It was a virtue that Menzies had praised earlier in his career, even if he did not always use the word. In the mid-1930s he had said, 'The first duty of every man is to do his utmost to stand on his own feet, to form his own judgements and to accept his own responsibilities.'[3] For Menzies the virtue of independence must animate any healthy democracy; it was no mere private virtue. Its very nature was relational, for the independent person was independent *from*, and this negative relationship was itself a form of service, for if one could stand on one's own two feet and support oneself then one was not a burden on others and one had the resources to fulfil one's duties to others. In that sense the virtue of independence was a negative duty that allowed the sturdy citizen to perform his positive duty to the community. In an undated speech entitled 'The ethics of popular self-government', Menzies argued that 'thrift, industry and independence are precious and vital elements in a balanced community life'.[4] He went on:

> The supreme test of the efficacy of democratic self-government is the national character. However perfect may be our mechanics of government, that government will have proved disastrous unless it encourages among its citizens the cardinal virtues of unselfishness, a broad and human charity as the Apostle Paul understood it, manly independence and the passionate love for true justice to all men.[5]

Menzies' early descriptions of the English character were very similar to Trevelyan's characterisation of nineteenth-century cultural puritanism quoted above. In a speech delivered in England in 1941, Menzies identified the first trait of the English as 'an instructive and unashamed religious sense', which Menzies called 'an instinct'. Much like Menzies' own Christianity, this was less a credal religion than a religion of conduct and instinct:

It is, you know, a sort of Hebrew element in our character.[6] It elevates the moral test of conduct and to that extent diminishes the intellectual test of conduct. It prefers the heart to the head; and, as we look around this world, this very vexed world of ours and we seek to determine why it is that so many millions of people are placing all their hope of the future on what the people of this country will do, we will find that the reason for that faith is not some belief in the dry detached intellectual powers of this country; it is a profound and instinctive belief in the courage and honesty of this country's heart.[7]

It was also out of this English character that Menzies thought political liberties could be derived. Some years earlier he privately noted: 'Again and again I come back to the conviction that in this "green and pleasant land" the essential elements of greatness are to be found ...' Menzies wrote of the English 'attachment to a belief that there is a moral order in the universe', but most importantly the English tendency to 'tolerance of other people's views and conduct ... [which] indicates a real and profound allegiance to the tradition of freedom of thought'.[8] All of these English instincts received their most eloquent expression by Menzies in his famous 1942 radio broadcasts.

Menzies' understanding that the English were attached to a 'moral order' is not far removed from W.K. Hancock's claim made in the 1930s that the English were moral because they were a medieval people who resisted the Machiavellianism of modernity, as exemplified by Nazism in Germany or fascism in Italy. The emphasis on character is instructive. Menzies does not consider that morality and freedom derive from theoretical constructions but from habit and custom. It is embodied in real life. This is very much in line with a long tradition of thought in English life and religion, dating back to Sir Thomas More and Richard Hooker, in which theoretical knowledge, in the sense of verbal formulations, is not as highly regarded as real knowledge as expressed through action.[9] Even the age's most profound thinkers repeated the tropes of Englishness; thus Santayana:

> Opinions, he feels, should be summary and safe; they should express the lessons of experience.
>
> As he conceives it at first, experience does not merely exist, it teaches. In a sporadic fashion it yields sound satisfactions, clear warnings, plain facts. It admonishes him to trust his senses, the reports of reputable travellers and naturalists, Christianity and the British constitution, all when duly revised; and on the other hand to shun popery, scholastic quibbles, absolutism and revolution.[10]

In its modern form, it is the tradition, beginning with Edmund Burke, traced by Raymond Williams in his *Culture and Society*.[11]

On Menzies' 1942 'Forgotten People' speech, Judith Brett has written of 'its roots in the debates between liberalism and Marxism'.[12] Admittedly, it is difficult to know just how much acquaintance Menzies had with Marxism as a political doctrine, or even with liberalism considered as a creed or theory, as opposed to a way of being in the world.[13] Although the 1942 speeches may have had their occasion in such ideological debates, the ideals in them cannot be contained within any textbook definition of liberalism. In 'The Forgotten People' Menzies was not entering into a theoretical debate but providing an expression of his understanding of the nature of freedom and its value in a world threatened by a brutal enemy. An illustration of this non-dogmatic approach is to be found in a work published at approximately the same time, W.K. Hancock's *Argument of Empire*. Hancock discusses freedom in the British Commonwealth/Empire as follows:

We do right to make certain far-reaching freedoms the target of our joint endeavour; we do right to claim them on behalf of our common humanity. But we must not expect that the kindreds and creeds of humanity will interpret them as we them, or use them as we use them. Some communities will value freedoms which we do not understand; some will not understand freedoms which we value. We must distinguish between spirit, form and substance. The spirit of freedom we hold to be universal; but the form of it must be appropriate to the substance of community life in its particular embodiment at particular periods of time. To force upon peoples forms of freedom for which they are not ready may wound the living freedom which they already possess.[14]

If we can speak of liberalism in Menzies' 'Forgotten People' speeches, it is essentially non-dogmatic and is the expression of a particular conception of the English tradition that he so admires.

Brett goes deeper and discusses the 'Protestant religious beliefs' that buttress much of his thought, particularly his emphasis on independence.[15] Although Brett's discussion of Weber's famous link between Protestantism and what C.B. Macpherson called 'possessive individualism' is well taken, 'the historical richness of the symbols Menzies is deploying against labour'[16] can be more definitely identified in terms of cultural puritanism as described. In particular, Menzies' tendency—also discussed by Brett[17]—is to distinguish people not so much on the grounds of economics but on moral grounds, or personal virtues.

Again, this can be seen as an unconscious recognition of what might be termed the Latin influence in English culture. Roman historians, including Livy and Sallust, understood history in moral terms. Individuals and peoples were to be understood in terms of their capacity to practise virtue on the one hand and the

moral defects of their character on the other. The rise and possible fall of Rome was to be understood in moral terms, and the
worst sin of all for Sallust is avarice. It saps independence and
virtue. There are powerful linkages between Roman moralism,
civic republicanism and puritanism in English life, and they are
mutually supportive.[18]

Britishness and duty

Once the British tradition of cultural puritanism is understood,
one can fully appreciate that Menzies was drawing on a tradition that stretched well beyond Australian shores. Indeed, Labor's
assault on the virtues that constituted cultural puritanism was the
central message of Menzies' 'Forgotten People' speeches: 'I have
been actively engaged in politics for fourteen years in the state of
Victoria and in the Commonwealth of Australia. In that period I
cannot readily recall many occasions upon which any policy was
pursued which was designed to help the thrifty, to encourage independence, to recognise the divine and valuable variations of men's
minds.'[19]

Sounding strangely Marxian, Menzies diagnosed the problem
to a large extent in terms of a lumpenbourgeoisie, which is 'for
the most part unorganised and unselfconscious'.[20] Throughout
Menzies' speeches he hangs the future well-being of Australia on
those—the middle class—who exemplify the puritan virtues that
are under attack from various fronts, national and global. The
middle class is described in puritan terms throughout his published
speeches. 'The spirit we need', said Menzies, is 'the spirit of sturdy
independence of the great middle class.'[21] These people 'urged on
by a spirit of independence, endeavour in spite of every parliamentary discouragement, to provide for their own future'. Menzies
could wax biblical, describing the middle class as 'the salt of the
earth' and saying that 'if the moral future of this country is to

be saved it must be saved by them'.[22] Again, it was 'those thrifty and independent people who count for so much in the solidity and progress of our country'.[23]

Yet these puritan virtues were not meant to be solely the preserve of the middle class. Menzies frequently applied them to his ideal vision of the nation as a whole:

> The best and strongest community is not that in which everybody looks to his neighbour hoping for something from him, but that in which everyone looks to his neighbour, willing and able to do something for him. In brief, we achieve the good of man when we help and encourage him to be a man—strong, self-reliant, intelligent, independent, sympathetic and generous.[24]

Or, '... the greatest element in a strong people is a fierce independence of spirit'.[25] Again: 'It all comes back to the sense of responsibility—that quiet and lovely virtue which can convert seven millions of individual people into a good and faithful community.'[26] This spirit of independence was strongly associated with that school of puritan values, the home.

In 'The Forgotten People', Menzies drew heavily upon the puritan ideal of domesticity, speaking of the three homes that, combined, secure the interests of the person ideally conceived: homes material, homes human and homes spiritual. By 'homes material' Menzies meant private property, although not private property as an outcome of the spirit of 'possessive individualism' but as a means to a loftier end: asylum; that is, a place 'to which we can withdraw, in which we can be among our friends, into which no stranger may come against our will'.[27]

By 'homes human' Menzies means not only family domesticity but also a private place in which parents can create independent citizens, incubators to produce 'lifters not leaners'. Scottish farmers sending their sons to Edinburgh University was his choice example. Rather than being content for their sons to work on the farm and expand the family wealth, the Scottish spirit was far more civic minded. For Menzies' ideal Scot, 'The great question is, "How can I qualify my son to help society?" Not, as we have so frequently thought, "How can I qualify society to help my son?"'[28]

Finally, by 'homes spiritual' Menzies meant not churches or even religion but what he called 'spirit'. By 'spirit' he meant 'a brave acceptance of unclouded individual responsibility'. Independence differed from individualism in that it was the self looking outward, not inward, and bound by duties to the wider community or the common good. Menzies could express the point rather epigrammatically: 'Human nature is at its greatest when it combines dependence upon God with independence of man.'[29] This independence was won by 'self sacrifice, by frugality and saving'.

Again, this emphasis on the home and the family as the foundation of the independent individual seems to be very Roman. Its focus is not so much religious belief and credal adherence as what the Romans termed *pietas*, a sense of reverence that manifests itself in fulfilling one's responsibilities to those around one. Augustus is praised by Suetonius for living a simple and frugal life. It is not so much about liberty in the negative sense as carrying out one's duties. It should be pointed out that, according to the idea of negative liberty, one has no duties or obligations—other than to obey the law; one is free to cultivate one's garden and to waste one's time as one pleases. In this sense, liberal individualism corrodes civic responsibility. Menzies would have been horrified by such a notion; homes and families were meant to produce individuals who possessed piety and recognised their responsibilities to those around them.

That Menzies could expect *all* Australians to practise the puritan virtues was owing to his cherished conception of what it was to be British, and Menzies stressed multiple times throughout his 1942 speeches that 'Australians are none the less good Australians because they are unhesitatingly British'.[30] When Menzies spoke of 'our race',[31] he was referring not so much to genetics as to a set of historically accumulated virtues whose collective uniqueness constituted the British character. Menzies' conception of Britishness was Whiggish and best embodied in the institution of the British parliamentary system and the virtues required for its effective operation. Typical of Menzies' panegyric to the British race—'a free people'—is the following:

> The truth is that ever since the wise men gathered about the village tree in the Anglo-Saxon village of early England, the notion of free self-government has run like a thread through our history. The struggle for freedom led an English Parliament to make war on its King and execute him at the seat of government, confined the kingship itself to a parliamentary domain, established the cabinet system and responsibility, set in place the twin foundation stones of the sovereignty of Parliament and the rule of law on which our whole civil edifice is built.[32]

His frequent descriptions of the British in wartime tended to concentrate on their stoicism and unflinching determination to carry on with life as normal. World War II was, for Menzies, a crisis that demanded the cultural puritanism that he feared was being lost or smothered in Australia.

Duty infused all of Menzies' political thought. Even his discussion of concepts such as freedom and rights was often conceived in terms of being on the flipside of duty. In 'The Forgotten People',

Menzies mentions 'freedom' once and 'independence' four times. Speaking of '*real* freedom', Menzies contrasts this with 'moral and intellectual refuge in the emotions of a crowd' as opposed to 'a brave acceptance of an unclouded individual responsibility' manifest in a commitment to 'self-sacrifice'.[33] This conception of freedom is a far cry from the negative conception of liberty that continues to animate classical liberalism and libertarianism. Even in the speeches discussing the 'Four Freedoms', Menzies is uncomfortable dwelling on the freedoms as individual liberties and quickly reminds his audience that these freedoms are for others as well as themselves and that, as such, our freedoms involve a duty to allow others to enjoy theirs.[34]

When discussing John Stuart Mill's 'harm principle', Menzies interprets it not as a liberty we have from the interference of the state but as a duty we have not to injure others. Indeed, 'The man who claims much aggressive liberty for himself may be getting it at the expense of somebody else'.[35] Typical of Menzies' unease with dwelling on freedom is the following:

> Freedom is not a commodity you buy over a counter. It is a principle of life. It must be strong to resist its enemies. It is a source of power, not something passive or dead. My right to be free imposes on me obligations of the most absolute kind to defend my freedom. And so if I am to have freedom from want I must pay the price of that freedom. I must work and strive.[36]

The same is true of the reign of liberty in the democratic system:

> If there is one thing that distinguishes the democratic system from the dictatorship system, it is that in our own casual and cheerful fashion we do believe in liberty. If you cross-examine

any one of us about what he believes, you will probably
discover that in the last resort he dislikes interference and
believes that, within decent limits, he should be allowed to
live his own life in his own way, provided that he does not
injure his neighbour, performs his social duty and is honest
and fair in the performance of his community duty.[37]

Thus, again, Menzies' discussion of liberty ends as a discussion of
duty and not the classical liberal—Millian—negative duty of not
harming others, but of a positive duty to contribute to one's society and community. In short, Menzies was little concerned with
freedom or liberty in the individualistic sense.

In many ways Menzies was barely concerned with defending
liberty beyond its defence as a prelude to a discussion of personal
responsibility, nicely captured in his conception of individuality,
not individualism. Much the same can be said about Menzies'
attitude to rights. Although he affirmed what we might call natural rights,[38] and that democracy is 'founded upon the rights of
the individual citizens',[39] Menzies was uncomfortable dwelling on
the topic of rights without drawing his readers' attention to their
attendant duties.[40]

As he did with independence, Menzies spoke of duty or responsibility as a quasi-religion, a civic credo necessary for a happy
country. In one of his most remarkable non-published speeches,
delivered two years after his 'Forgotten People' speech, he defined
the Christian gospel in civic–ethical terms as 'imposing on every
citizen the obligation of unselfishness, of thinking of the interests of his neighbour before his own and regarding himself as his
brother's keeper'. Yet, because citizens are selfish, politicians are
forced to appeal to citizens' 'devotion to material self-interest'.
But, he went on, 'if he were talking to an unselfish electorate, he
might talk in a different way'.[41]

You see there is the philosophy of responsibility and if every Australian said to himself repentedly, 'This business of building a New Jerusalem in Australia, this business of bringing into this community the Kingdom of God upon earth, is my business, not somebody else's'—if every Australian said this, Australia would be the wisest and happiest of all countries. We would instantaneously have OUR new age; because in a country in which everybody accepts all the responsibilities of life there can be no injustice. Do we accept these responsibilities? It is a great and a Christian virtue, you know, to accept responsibility; and if ever a man stood on earth and faced responsibility with courage, it was the Founder of our Faith.[42]

As always, Menzies was then quick to assure his audience that Australians did not measure up to this civic gospel; in fact, they perfectly measured up to Hancock's description of them as self-centred and dependent on that 'vast public utility'.

Individualism, individuality and citizenship

Thus, Menzies was not an individualist in any atomistic sense of that word and rarely praised 'individualism'.[43] Yet he spoke very frequently of the individual. It was 'individuality' rather than individualism that Menzies thought worth preserving. In many ways Menzies' concept of individuality resembled the idealist concept of personality. Personality was discussed at length in F.G. Eggleston's *Search for a Social Philosophy* (1941). Eggleston, like Menzies, spoke against the temptation to cast off individual responsibility for the comfort of group servility. In the midst of the increasing complexity of modern industrial society and with the totalitarian comforts of 'modern systems of power', 'Man', said Eggleston, 'becomes frightened and attaches himself to one or other of them; afraid of the moral responsibilities, of which his personality is making him dimply aware, he shelters behind some great non-moral aggregation.'[44] This imperative of personality to remain free from suffocating conformity ought ultimately to drive the individual outward rather than inward. As with the case of Menzies' individuality, Eggleston's personality was integrated into a Christian matrix of duties rather than rights:

> The Christian ethic attaches supreme value to personality; the life of each man is sacred; the hairs of our heads are numbered; no one falls without it being known. This is the obvious corollary of the doctrines of the good neighbour and means sympathetic recognition of all human personality. Thus all conventions or individual conduct which depress or destroy human personality are unchristian.[45]

Menzies' political vision was essentially an exposition of the last sentence of the above quote, which, for Menzies, applied especially to socialism. In 'The Forgotten People', speaking of the 'mass of unskilled people', Menzies assured his listeners that 'one of the prime objects of modern social and political policy is to give them a proper measure of security and provide the conditions which will enable them to acquire skill and knowledge and individuality'.[46] Like Eggleston, Menzies saw the economic implications of this in terms of a middle ground between 'selfish' *laissez-faire* capitalism and suffocating state socialism. The task was to 'keep the good elements of the capitalist system' while 'imposing upon capital the most stringent obligations to discharge its social and industrial duty'. Putting it more grandly: 'The great race of men is that one in which each individual develops his fullest individuality, in which ambition is encouraged, in which there are rewards for the courageous and enterprising, in which there is no foolish doctrine of equality between the active and the idle, the intelligent and the dull, the frugal and the improvident.'[47]

Individuality was, for Menzies, tightly bound up with his conception of democracy and freedom, 'for true democracy requires that the individual should think for himself, suffer for himself, act and vote according to his own judgment and on his own responsibility'. Making a rare positive reference to 'rights', Menzies described the 'rights of democratic man' as the right of 'every human soul—which is also an immortal soul—to reach its full development'.[48] Note here that Menzies' conception of rights is no mere individualistic preference satisfaction theory but a right to fulfil one's duty to self-development and independence.

The theory of citizenship[49] emerging from Menzies' conception of individuality is best described as puritan democracy; that is, a democracy of duties over rights grounded in a vision of the citizen as an immortal soul rather than a vector of interests. Menzies tended to refer to the virtues of independent man as 'spirit'. It is precisely this lack of spirit that Menzies spent much of his career warning Australians of. Indeed, this spiritlessness was, for Menzies, the chief threat to democracy. Democracy—its nature and its health—was a principal theme in the speeches collected in the 1943 volume *The Forgotten People*, whose subtitle was *And Other Studies in Democracy*. That 'The Forgotten People' speech refers to the contribution of the middle class to the health of democracy affirms that the 'and other' in the book's subtitle understands 'The Forgotten People' to be an essay about the cultural (puritan) preconditions of a healthy democracy as much as anything else.

Much like Walter Murdoch before him, Menzies' conception of citizenship had little to say about rights—Menzies rarely used the word in any positive sense, preferring 'liberties' or 'freedoms'—and focused on duties.[50] Menzies had stated as much in previous speeches: '[T]he social contract which binds any society together is one expressed primarily in terms of duties and of obligations.'[51] It shaped the view of democracy offered in Menzies' 1942 speeches.

Speaking of a 'true conception of democracy', Menzies expressed his view in language touched by the Christian idealist language of the time. Rather than conceiving the essence of democracy in terms of a procedure or 'machine', Menzies reaffirmed his vision of democracy's essence as 'spirit', a spirit that 'adjusts man to man':

> Now, if this spirit is of the essence of democracy, can we rightly say that we have understood or practised it? For, if man is to be adjusted to man, if we are to live together in mutual amity and justice, if we are to be dignified without being proud or overbearing, we must be givers rather than receivers; we must be quick to discharge our duties and modest about our rights. For the harmony and brotherly love of a family is not maintained on a basis of claims. In the wise language of the Bible, the family are 'in honour preferring one another'.[52]

The puritan tone continued, as 'our first task as professing democrats is to examine both our faith and ourselves'.[53]

Self-examination was a ubiquitous theme in puritan devotion and no doubt would have been present in Menzies' Methodist–Presbyterian upbringing. Such scrutiny leads to an uncomfortable truth: 'That we have all too frequently forgotten the duties which attach to free citizenship cannot be denied.'[54] In discussing the democratic ideal of citizenship, Menzies repeated the puritan tropes: 'I do not want my children and their children to be dependants upon the State …'[55] 'What is the good of man?' asked Menzies: '[W]e achieve the good of man when we help and encourage him to be a man—strong, self-reliant, intelligent, independent, sympathetic and generous.'[56] How do we create such citizens? Menzies' answer was remarkably secular, given his frequent allusions to Christianity: education. Universities were Menzies' churches.[57]

'We must train for citizenship', said Menzies. As idealist social philosophers had been saying for decades, technology without morality renders life more dangerous. Thus, 'To develop every human being to his fullest capacity of thought, for action, for sacrifice and for endurance is our major task ...'[58] Central to Menzies' ideal of democratic citizenship therefore was spirit, which he conceptualised in terms of sturdy independence and sacrifice. Echoing the more Christian expression of citizenship that flourished during World War II in Australia, Great Britain and America, Menzies spoke of the 'golden rule of citizenship': that 'each of us should act as he would wish all other citizens to act'. The puritan emphasis on self-scrutiny applied to this citizenship, as 'every citizen must test this matter for himself and be earnest to discover his own duty'.[59] Employing biblical imagery and concepts, Menzies described his ideal middle-class citizens—those 'urged on by a spirit of independence'—as the 'salt of the earth' and believed that 'if the moral future of this country is to be saved it must be saved by them'.[60]

Indeed, Menzies' conception of good citizenship was expressed in moral terms that eschewed rights talk but had a particularly puritan inflection. The limits of freedom were not determined by the 'rights' of others but were to be exercised within 'decent limits'[61] or 'within the proper limits of decency'.[62] 'Decency' went well beyond Mill's harm principle, for the decent citizen 'should be allowed to live his own life in his own way, provided that he does not injure his neighbour, performs his social duty and is honest and fair in the performance of his community duty'.[63] This was all part of Menzies' diatribe against the 'vast public utility' view of the state so well described by Hancock and redescribed by Menzies as 'the idle and false doctrine that the Government owes us everything while we owe the Government nothing'.[64] The 'independent man' was to be set against his anti-type; that is, those who 'clamour for their so-called "rights"' and who 'dodge every civic responsibility'; such are 'poor democrats'.[65] Via the 'spirit of sturdy independence' the 'great middle class' would reconsecrate an increasingly individualistic society.[66]

The problem of materialism

Menzies could oscillate between idealist and puritan language at times. Like most commentators touched by idealism, Menzies could describe the present world crisis not merely in terms of a fight for 'all the rights of democratic man' but as a struggle for 'the right of every human soul—which is an immortal soul—to reach its full development'. Puritan references were never far away. On the same page Menzies referred to 'a Scots Presbyterian preacher' who, to Menzies' satisfaction, pointed out that 'progress had never depended upon the ideas produced by the majority'.[67] Elsewhere again, Menzies could wax lofty, praising the 'vital moral element in the community which produces an utter willingness to share in sacrifice and effort'. He could then urge his listeners on to 'a ruthless self-examination', asking: 'Are there thousands of us who have no conception of discipline as self-discipline, but who respond only to some authority from outside ourselves?'[68]

Idealist social theorists were not only critical of the more brutal materialism of communist regimes; they were also just as critical of the materialism of capitalist democracies. Idealists judged both forms of social organisation as dehumanising, although obviously in different ways. Such theorists tended to see the ends of the government and the economy in terms of individual 'personality' or a kind of human flourishing existing within preordained moral boundaries; certainly not reducible to mere preference satisfaction, as utilitarians tended to argue. Thus, Eggleston wrote,

'In the unfortunate circumstances of our times we are bound to fight against all systems which seek to enslave the human spirit and prevent the development of personality in its highest form.'[69] This talk of spirit was also widely adopted by Menzies and was central to his theory of democracy: 'In my own opinion, our most grievous error has been that we have thought too much of democracy in mechanical terms—as a system of government—and too little of it as a spirit, a moving force; not a mere vehicle for the expression of the human mind alone, but a challenge to the human spirit.'[70]

Menzies' speeches on democracy were full of such sentiments, usually infused with explicitly Christian references that would have resonated with British Australians at the time, for World War II encouraged a revival of the sentiment—famously expressed by Churchill's 'Battle of Britain' speech of June 1940[71]—that British society and civilisation was Christian. This was most evident in England's Education Act (1944), which reintroduced Christian religious teaching into moral class hours in schools. The Act was praised by Menzies, who couched his own attempt to intro-duce religious instruction into Victorian education in terms of a declining ethic of duty:

Nobody can suppose that we are educating our children, except for disaster, by turning them out of purely secular establishments at the age of fourteen, fifteen or sixteen years, merely educated to a point at which they think there is nothing left for them to learn, aggressively conscious of what they suppose to be their rights and oblivious of that penetrating feeling of moral obligation to others, which alone can make a community of men successful.[72]

There has been a tendency to focus on what might be described as the 'political essays' of *The Forgotten People*. It is the case, however, that some of the other essays provide considerable insight to Menzies' moral personality. In his broadcast on the moral element in total war, Menzies emphasised the need to believe in a moral creed to provide the impetus for the people of Australia to strive to win the war. He seems to have a fear that many Australians lacked a strong sense of good and evil and were perhaps motivated to act essentially by individual self-interest. Such a view is not so different from Eggleston's portrayal of the 'self-contained' man who has imperfectly developed his individuality. In fact, the war produced a number of works, including the *Think or Be Damned* series edited by Brian Penton, which were critical of Australian civic practice.[73] In many ways, this desire for strong moral belief can be seen as a criticism of what many have identified as the utilitarian creed of Australia and its thin set of morals. Hence Menzies argued:

> There can be no passionate patriotism or willing self-sacrifice in war unless we know in our hearts that we are fighting for good things against evil things and there can be no better world order except on a moral basis. The brain of man may devise wonders and the hand of man execute them, but they will all fall into evil and harmful uses unless the heart of man—the guide of conduct—is sound and true. This is true whatever systems we may choose for the accomplishment of our ends.
>
> Capitalism cannot rebuild the world aright except on a basis of humane and enlightened responsibility to the community.[74]

Even more interesting is the way in which Menzies argued that if one was to win the war, a purely materialist outlook, such as was advocated by Karl Marx, was not sufficient for a worthy peace. In a remarkable passage, Menzies notes: '[T]he Russian people have developed on top of the Marxian doctrines a burning spirit of faith and determination as far removed from materialism as the earth is from the sun.'[75] If Australia is to succeed, it needed also to develop a proper spiritual outlook that would give it the determination it needed if the war was to be won. Hence he recognises that 'the resurgence of Germany as a terrific military power is largely to be attributed to Hitler's youth movement and to the burning belief that it acquired and preached in its leader, its nation and its destiny'.[76] Its moral passion may be evil, but it cannot be countered by those who have no moral passion. The enemy in Australia was the self-contained man who thought in terms of narrow self-interest. Hence, Menzies concludes: 'No longer would the question be, "How much can I get?" or "How little can I do?" but, "What can I give?" or, in the immortal words, "What can I do to be saved?"'[77]

Menzies' views on the use of hatred as an instrument of war policy equally provides a window into his moral universe. Menzies is adamant that 'It is, in my opinion, poor policy to try to persuade people to despise the Japanese'.[78] Menzies' refusal to engage in hatred is also reflected in his opposition to sectarian hatred. He refused to be governed by hatred and would not countenance glorifying it and turning it 'into something which ought to be cultivated and made a sort of chronic state of mind'.[79] He rejected the notion that 'Australian civilians are so lacking in the true spirit of citizenship that they need to be filled artificially with a spirit of hatred before they will do their duty to themselves and to those who are fighting for them'.[80]

He seems to have feared that a genuine patriotism could be replaced by a basic human emotion such as hatred. This would fit in nicely with Menzies' concern that there was a lack of genuine moral passion in Australia, and one could draw the conclusion that, in the absence of such passion, basic emotion would fill the void. His crucial argument was that the war would eventually have to be succeeded by peace. Enmity would eventually need to give place to amity and peace. There can be no doubt that in his heart of hearts Menzies was a man of peace. His views on the coming of peace are worth quoting in full:

> Peace must not only close the door on war; it must open the door to better things. It is not by treaty that we shall pass out of this hideous valley of death into the higher lands of peace and goodwill. Peace may be all sorts of things—a real end of war, a mere exhaustion, an armed interlude before the next struggle. But it will only be by a profound stirring in the hearts of men that we shall reach goodwill.
>
> In short, when this war is over we all hope to live in a better world in which both Germans and Japanese, violently purged of their lust for material power, will be able to live and move in amity with ourselves and in that friendly intercourse which is a more powerful instrument of peace than any artificial plan ever devised.[81]

War was now, and it was essential that the war be won. What needed to be avoided was to take 'the honest and natural and passing passions of the human heart and degrade them into sinister and bitter policy'.[82] War was but a phase, and if Australia was to fight the war as it should be fought,

> We shall, in other words, do well if we leave the dignity and essential nobility of our cause unstained and get on urgently with the business of so working, so fighting and so sacrificing ourselves that the cause emerges triumphant and the healing benefits of its success become available as a blessing not merely for us but for all mankind.[83]

Another aspect of Menzies' moral outlook is illustrated by his broadcast on 'The Drink Problem'. Commenting on what appears to be an increase in alcohol consumption during the war, Menzies demonstrates that he is no wowser opposed to the consumption of alcohol, nor a believer in 'a sudden degeneration of the character of the average citizen'.[84] For Menzies, the excessive consumption of alcohol is simply a symptom of the changes wrought by a combination of an increase of money in the economy and the impact of rationing of many items. Menzies' solution is to treat alcohol in the same way as any other commodity and restrict its availability. Nevertheless the objective of taking such action will be moral: 'There must be a compulsion to frugality and when we have frugality, intemperance and extravagance will automatically be subdued.'[85] Frugality, along with self-discipline, is something to be encouraged. Such rhetoric falls squarely within the puritan moral paradigm, whose emphasis was autonomy via self-restraint; autonomy as mastery over vice and sin.

This reading of Menzies' 1942 'Forgotten People' and the speeches published the following year does not reject the notion that Menzies had an identifiable approach to political questions that was consistent with, or that at times resonated with, tropes and ideals typical of liberalism and conservatism. What we question is the notion that Menzies can be reduced to either liberalism or conservatism, or even be simply described as a liberal conservative in a way that fully captures what he was trying to do when he discussed the issues of his time. In fact Menzies was the embodiment of a particular kind of Britishness that was capacious enough to host both liberal and conservative tropes but which ultimately resonated most with the cultural puritanism that was so central to the British identity that informed Menzies' early years.

Who were Menzies' 'Forgotten People'? Indeed, the middle class, but really those who Menzies thought most embodied the spirit of puritanism as he had been brought up to think about it and whose death social commentators since the late nineteenth century had been lamenting. Menzies' 'Forgotten People' speech was the greatest expression of his heroic attempt to revive cultural puritanism in a rapidly changing Australia, itself becoming more integrated into a rapidly changing world.

4

CHRISTIANITY, DEMOCRACY AND CIVILISATION

But a true conception of democracy goes even beyond this, for democracy is more than a machine; it is a spirit. It is based upon the Christian conception that there is in every human soul a spark of the divine; that, with all their inequalities of mind and body, the souls of men stand equal in the sight of God.

Menzies, 'The nature of democracy'

Menzies' political thought is not reducible to textbook liberalism or conservatism, even liberal conservatism, or vice versa. His project was one of cultural restoration, even if the culture he sought to restore never really typified all Australians or Britons in the first place. But certain expressions of this cultural puritanism, as we saw above, cohered nicely with conservative and liberal approaches to society and politics. In this sense Menzies—at least before the Cold War—was a cultural puritan first and foremost and anything else in consequence.

Edmund Burke himself embodied something like this, being neither Tory nor Whig, but standing for a tradition that could to a large degree accommodate either. Burkean tropes ornamented

Menzies' speeches and publications throughout his entire life. '[The] greatest aim in public affairs', declared Menzies in Westminster Parliament in 1935, 'is to preserve everything we have that is good.'[1] After visiting the Magna Carta on the same trip to England, Menzies was overwhelmed:

> What a day! I have literally been in the presence of the Great Charter among the barons assembled at Runnymede; I have seen the very handwriting of the man whose sword and character and mind made England a free country. I have stood where stood many times the great John Hampden and have sat awhile in the invisible presence of the greatest poet of liberty. How could any Englishman tear down the temple built by these great hands? The survival of a free Parliament in this land is not to be marvelled at. *One realises that a Parliament for England is no mere result or adoption of a political theory (as it was on the Continent) but something growing from the very roots of the English life.*[2]

The conservative sense of continuity was something that Menzies even in the mid-1960s thought characterised the English pathos. He saw it in the long procession of youths who solemnly came to pay their respects at the funeral of Sir Winston Churchill. It was a display he described in sacred terms. According to Menzies, 'This is the continuing city in reality that is referred to in the Bible and it is a great characteristic, particularly of our own people ...'[3]

Menzies self-consciously described himself as a liberal. Partly this is because the fundamental political divide in Australia is not Liberal/Conservative but ALP/non-ALP. There was no precedent in Australian political terms for adopting the label 'conservative'; in fact to do so would be political poison. The key issue was to identify a party as being opposed to socialism and the desire for the state to own and operate industries. Hence Menzies wrote: 'We took the name "Liberal" because we were determined to be a progressive party, willing to make experiments, in no sense reactionary but believing in the individual, his rights and his enterprise, and rejecting the socialist panacea.'[4]

Menzies was aware of the difference in meaning between North America and England and Australia in the use of the word 'liberal':

> In the United States of America, the word 'liberal' is used in contradistinction to 'conservative', but it seems, in recent years, to have acquired a special connotation. When I resided in America for some months in 1966–7, I thought that it threatened to become a word which had special reference to racial relations; to 'civil rights'; to the vexed questions of 'integration' and 'segregation'.[5]

He also did not see an Australian Liberal Party as in any way analogous to the English Liberal Party. Menzies was correct. The Australian Liberal Party and liberalism in Australia is *sui generis*, a product of the particular conditions that have operated in Australia.

In this way Menzies can be seen to have adopted a Burkean approach to politics. He was a liberal but not a dogmatic liberal. He believed in the individual but not some ethereal individual understood in a mechanical sense as an entity who would fulfil his or her function according to some predetermined economic model. It was real individuals and their families that stood at the centre of Menzies' approach to politics. Hence he praised the English tradition because it rejected the abstract and deductive approach to law and politics in favour of an inductive and empirical approach.

Menzies supported the idea of the individual, real flesh and blood individuals who attempt to make their way in the world. This can be seen in his famous radio broadcast of 1942 on the 'forgotten people'. Having lost office in 1941 and with the non-Labor side of politics in total disarray, Menzies sought to set out his political and social beliefs and values in these broadcasts. This was a deliberate and targeted approach to what Menzies called the Middle Class, but it was no bourgeoisie in the European sense. It excluded both the rich and the unskilled, although it did include 'salary-earners, shopkeepers, skilled artisans, professional men and women, farmers and so on'. These were individuals who strove to build a better life for themselves, to own their own home and pursue honest ambition. They are the people who have a 'stake in the country'.[6]

Moreover, for Menzies at the centre of this 'stake in the country' is home and family, individuals who have 'responsibility for homes—homes material, homes human and homes spiritual'. What emerges from the speeches making up *The Forgotten People* and Menzies' other writings is a fairly simple, almost homespun political vision of human beings, their desires and aspirations, expressed in clear English. 'The home', stated Menzies, 'is the foundation of sanity and sobriety; it is the indispensable condition of continuity; its health determines the health of society as a whole.'[7]

The material home represents the concrete expression of the habits of frugality and saving 'for a home of our own'. The human home centres on the family and the desire to do the best for it: 'My home is where my wife and children are. The instinct to be with them is the great instinct of civilised man; the instinct to give them a chance in life—to make them not leaners but lifters—is a noble instinct.'[8]

But this is not a purely materialistic vision of the individual involved merely in getting and spending as a means of physical improvement. It has an equally important spiritual dimension; hence Menzies continues, 'Human nature is at its greatest when it combines dependence upon God with independence of man.'[9] Part of this spiritual dimension displays his Scottish ancestry in his proud invocation of the spirit of independence: 'The greatest element in a strong people is a fierce independence of spirit. This is the only real freedom and it has as its corollary a brave acceptance of unclouded individual responsibility.'[10]

This is not a liberalism rooted in an economic vision of the world. It certainly believes in ambition and the desire to achieve and 'get ahead'. This is tempered, however, by recognition that human beings also have a willingness to serve and to give, which is a central element of human ambition. Menzies was no utilitarian, and he was severely critical of utilitarianism as a philosophy. The ideal individual in Menzies' eyes was far from being someone who maximised utility. His vision of the individual came from religion; his Scottish heritage, which placed a great emphasis on education; a desire to excel and achieve; and a belief that individuals have a responsibility to use their talents and capacities to benefit others. It is the vision of the professional—and Menzies was of course a talented lawyer— rather than that of the businessman or the economist.

In the Australian context, this form of liberalism looks back to a nineteenth-century tradition of what could be termed aristocratic liberalism and the idea that democratic communities produced 'natural aristocracies' that would rule for the benefit of the whole community.[11] According to this tradition, liberalism essentially meant good government, a form of government under which the individual could flourish. It was profoundly Burkean in that it rested firmly on the trustee model of representation and the idea that representatives were not bound to do as their constituents bid them. They acted in the best interests of the whole community. This was in sharp distinction to the system of representation developed by the Australian Labor Party whereby representatives were essentially delegates of the party and bound to do as the extra-parliamentary party organisation demanded. Policy was created by the party conference, and members were bound to follow that policy regardless of circumstance, what their consciences told them or the common good.[12]

Menzies clearly stood in the lineage of this form of Australian aristocratic liberalism. It was members of this tradition who had created the Commonwealth constitution that came into being in 1901. An examination of the constitutional debates of the 1890s reveals many Burkean themes, including an aversion to theoretical approaches to constitution making and a desire to adapt existing institutions rather than to create new structures based on mechanical principles. At the same time, many of the speakers endorsed aristocratic liberalism and the freedom of parliamentary representatives to take decisions within parliament without reference to outside forces. Hence Bernhard Wise, a well-known advocate of what today would be termed social liberalism, spoke against the use of the referendum as a constraint on the member and a transfer of power from the informed to the ignorant.[13]

Menzies and the art of politics

This great concern for the dignity of parliament and its members was also clearly at the forefront of Menzies' understanding of politics and the way it should be conducted. Menzies had a clear-cut understanding of the role of Parliament and the role of the elected representatives, which owed much to Burke. Part of this Burkean understanding of politics had been transmitted to Victoria, Menzies' home state, by William Hearn, appointed as professor to the University of Melbourne in the 1850s, in his work on English government.[14] Menzies' appreciation of the proper role of the parliamentary representative can be seen in the following discussion:

[W]e have increasingly misunderstood and debased the function of a member of Parliament. We have treated him as a paid delegate to run our errands and obey our wishes and not as a representative, bound, as Edmund Burke so nobly said, to bring his 'matured judgement' to the service of his electors. We encourage our members of Parliament to tremble at the thought of a hostile public meeting and expect them to flutter in the breeze caused by thousands of printed forms demanding this or that and signed with suitable threats by carefully canvassed voters.

Quite bluntly, if you want paid agents, hired men, bound to do your bidding even when they know or believe that you are wrong, anxious at all costs to keep your favour, their eyes turned always towards the next election, then you will get a Parliament of the spineless and democracy will disappear. For political systems have much more frequently been overthrown by their own corruption and decay than by external forces.[15]

Menzies attacked the delegate model of representation and the idea that 'the function of their member of Parliament is to ascertain, if he can, what a majority of his electors desire and then plump for it in Parliament'. He called it a 'stupid and humiliating conception of the function of the member of Parliament'.[16]

Menzies clearly believed in the positive role of the Member of Parliament as much more than just a mouthpiece of the people. The member was in a real sense an 'aristocrat' in the original meaning of the word:

The true function of a member of Parliament is to serve his electors not only with his vote but with his intelligence. If some problem arises in Parliament about which he has knowledge and to which he has devoted his best thought, how absurd it would be—indeed how dangerous it would be—if he should allow his considered conclusion to be upset by a temporary clamour by thousands of people, most of whom in the nature of things could not have his sources of information and have probably in any event not thought the problem out at all.[17]

Politics was a noble calling and one in which individuals should seek to participate. It was central to the life of any community. Unlike many twenty-first-century liberals, Menzies did not see political action as a necessary evil to be avoided whenever possible, only resorted to when the laws of nature failed. Politics was an essential element of any community and required a group of talented and knowledgeable individuals to conduct it. Certainly this resonates with much civic republicanism, but to the extent to which civic republicanism was part of English character.[18] More importantly, it was an honourable calling that individuals of ability should follow for the benefit of their fellow human beings.

That, briefly stated, is why I believe that politics is the most important and responsible civil activity to which a man may devote his character, his talents and his energy. We must, in our own interests, elevate politics into statesmanship and statecraft. We must aim at a condition of affairs in which we shall no longer reserve the dignified name of statesman for a Churchill or a Roosevelt, but extend it to lesser men who give honourable and patriotic service in public affairs.[19]

From this point of view politics always trumps economics. The role of the politician is to work for the common good, not to conduct the affairs of the country according to the abstract laws of economics. This helps to explain the emphasis that Menzies placed on politics as an art. While he did not reject that there was a certain imperfect science attached to politics, it was the practice of politicians, its 'art', that made politics politics:

> We have neglected it as an art, the delineating and practice of *how* and *when* to do these things and above all, how to persuade a self-governing people to accept and loyally observe them. This neglect is of crucial importance, for I am prepared to assert that it is only if the art of politics succeeds that the science of politics will be efficiently studied and mastered.[20]

Menzies' essentially Burkean approach to politics and political action also calls to mind certain of the ideas of Michael Oakeshott. If politics is an art, it requires an artist schooled in its techniques to practise it. These practitioners embody the role of the representative as a leader in a democratic society:

> Finally, if the democratic politician is really to understand the importance of his art and practice it, he must be a leader. It is still as true as it was when Edmund Burke said it, that a Member of Parliament is not a delegate but a representative, bound to bring not merely his vote but his judgement to the service of his people. Just as a democracy cannot be preserved in war without a great and prevailing physical courage, so it cannot be wisely governed and preserved in peace without moral courage.[21]

Menzies placed an enormous importance on the role of speech as a crucial element of the proper working of such a democratic society. He claimed that he always wrote his own speeches but was scornful of the idea that a political leader should simply present a speech that was already written out. He disliked the 'innovation' of the use of the microphone at political meetings.[22] He was famous for using interjectors as a means of firing up the delivery of his speeches. Although he never discusses the topic in this way, one suspects that Menzies believed that there was a sort of organic relationship between a representative and his or her constituents that was largely conducted through the medium of speech-making in public meetings. Certainly he placed speech-making at the centre of political activity, as the means through which a political leader explained to constituents why certain actions had been taken.

Finally, Menzies was a sincere democrat but not a populist democrat who pandered to the views of what he saw as the not particularly well-informed populace. He was a Burkean democrat who placed enormous emphasis on the public role of the elected representative. He rejected a mechanical approach to politics; for him, democracy was not about a formal set of arrangements but the spirit of humanity, just as homes material made no sense without homes spiritual. As a true liberal and conservative in the English tradition, for Menzies the ultimate objective of politics was the individual considered as a spiritual being:

> But a true conception of democracy goes even beyond this, for democracy is more than a machine; it is a spirit. It is based upon the Christian conception that there is in every human soul a spark of the divine; that, with all their inequalities of mind and body, the souls of men stand equal in the sight of God. So it is that, while Fascists and Nazis concentrate their efforts upon the power of the State, regarding the citizen as the mere minister to that power, democrats must concern themselves with what they see to be the true end and final justification of the State; the chief end of the State becomes man—man the individual, man the immortal spirit.[23]

Bridging the sacred and the secular

What might be termed a religious spirit coloured everything that Menzies wrote about politics. Human beings were not material entities; they were not to be understood in mechanical terms. They were much more:

> With all our modern cleverness—with our wireless waves and aeroplanes and almost thinking machines—we are still only on the fringes of the universe of thought. We grope out towards the light, seeing an occasional flash of beauty or of understanding, hearing occasionally the penetrating voice of reason. Civilisation is in the heart and mind of man, not in the work of his hands. And in the heart of every man, whatever he may call himself, is that instinct to touch the unknown, to know what comes after, to see the invisible.[24]

An idealist spirit infused most of what he had to say about democracy and civilisation—two issues that most exercised those touched by the idealist tradition. Menzies' Christianity was sincere but not evangelical. Although some of Menzies' contemporaries, like G.V. Portus, definitely abandoned their Christian faith for a more rational idealism,[25] others, like Eggleston and Menzies, liberalised it to varying degrees and integrated it into their broader social philosophy. This was very much in keeping with idealism more generally. Unlike his father, Menzies was no enthusiast, and his private travel diary written during 1935 reveals a mildly liberal Christianity.[26] Menzies rarely had a positive thing to record about the church sermons that he heard while on tour in England. In his private diary he occasionally comments on them:

> April 25th Anzac Day service: 'A poor Service, with a posturing parson in the pulpit—the sort of preacher who is

"full of sound and fury, signifying nothing" and has a mind like a jumble sale.'[27]

5th May: 'Go into Hyde Park to hear the orators at the Marble Arch end. Large, good-natured and curious crowds and every variety of gospel. An old Bible expounder— Salvation Army (resorting, wisely, to songs rather than speeches)—a "Protestant Truth" man, humourless and fanatical. (Why? Is Protestantism inconsistent with a sense of humour?) ... A "Catholic Evidence Guild" stand, with an ascetic-looking priest (McNab) in cassock and gown ... A sort of Catholic Bishop of England with great wit and a sort of spurious scholarship vastly attractive to a large crowd. I am, on the whole, depressed because once more I discover that the only views commonly stated in public with brightness and subtlety are those which I don't hold.'[28]

The best he could offer was a backhanded compliment to an 'old vicar', who 'mumbles the service in the usual meaningless way, but preaches quite vigorously, his statement that the literal inter- pretation of the Bible was now abandoned "by all intelligent men, including most of the bishops" being much appreciated by me'.[29]

At the same time his diary is ornamented from beginning to end with accounts of the historic churches he visited in his travels throughout England.[30] Indeed, the trope of the church and cathe- dral—important for cultural puritanism[31]—frequently appeared in Menzies' idyllic descriptions of 'Englishness'. A sketch of a church building would eventually feature in a Liberal Party elec- tion pamphlet.[32]

Menzies' religion was moral and aesthetic, with little reference to credal dogma. His understanding of Christianity is of a spiritual force immanent within the British people and expressing itself in their way of life. Liberal Anglicanism, building on the fact that the

Church of England was defined less by a creed than by its practices as set out in the *Book of Common Prayer*, had accentuated this tendency, especially as the English grappled with the place of religion in a world that was being shaped by Enlightenment modernity and by the discovery of the plurality of world religions. In these circumstances, for many intelligent people, ethics and piety came to count for much more than the verbal formulations that they recited as an affirmation of their belief.

He seems to have imagined the country Englishmen as the ideal, their lives and character infused with duties sacred and secular:

Across the valley is the spire of a Church, erected by a former owner to celebrate his winning of the Derby. The English county families see no incongruity in this, for their domestic life is compounded hamoniously of the sacred and the secular. They give each man his due and give each thing its share of interest. Their notion of a real man is perhaps not a bad one; he must dress well, but comfortably; he must be interested in public affairs, but not officious; he must be intelligent but without making too much of a point of it; he must attend to the rites of the Church, but leave the public discussion of religion to the Nonconformists; if he quotes poetry to you (which he sometimes does) it is in a shamefaced way in a quiet corner of the garden; he is rather of opinion that it is better to ride boldly to hounds than to face up to a stiff problem of the intellect; and in the last crisis of emergency he fights or works or dies for his country with as much nonchalance as if he were keeping a tea engagement.[33]

No doubt Menzies is to some extent also describing himself here; a sacro-secular religion of duty, light on dogma—at least publicly stated dogma—and a distance from evangelicals.

Although Menzies was himself no evangelical, he may have had a grudging admiration for their energy, and on occasion lamented that that energy had been lost from much of the Church of England. Speaking of a service he attended at Canterbury Cathedral:

> The Service, to be frank, possesses that cold mechanical tone so chronic in English services. The Archbishop once more (as at St Paul's) fails to rise to the occasion—his great abilities are not exhibited in the pulpit. There is something wrong with the churches here; the Church of England seems to lack all evangelical fire and the fire of the Free Churches develop heat and not light.[34]

Menzies could at times be encouraged by the overt displays of religious fervour offered by the English, but mainly because he saw religious sincerity as the greatest bulwark against communism.[35] It is not entirely clear whether Menzies connected the 'lack of evangelical fire' in the Church of England with a broader trend of secularisation that was being noticed at the time. Although the cultural deposit of the zealous religion of the later nineteenth century was still strong and evident in the 1920s and 1930s,[36] some social commentators such as Dean Inge saw English religiosity as a train still in motion but slowing down, for its fuel had been exhausted earlier down the track. Speaking of 'organised religious bodies losing ground', according to Inge in 1926, there seemed 'no hope of [it] being halted'.[37] Menzies himself could at times reflect on the hollowness of much of the religion of his age. When visiting the tomb of Tutankhamen in 1935, he marvelled at the faith of the Egyptians in the afterlife and compared it with his own age's propensity to store riches on Earth.[38]

The age from which the historic Puritan movement of the sixteenth and seventeenth centuries arose drew no lines of distinction between the sacred and the secular, or, at least, refused to compart-mentalise them in real life—hence the much-studied relationship between historic puritanism and secular politics.[39] The same held for cultural Puritanism, with its emphasis on public Sabbath observance, civic activism and moral reform. Hence the fusion of Christianity and civilisation in Menzies' public thought, which also resembled much idealist thought in England and Australia.[40]

Menzies' approach to rescuing civilisation—or, less ambi-tiously, Australian society—from the malaise of spirit operated within a more general understanding of the relationship between the sacred and the secular. He could say to the congregation of a Presbyterian church in Woollahra in 1944 that, '[I]f there is one thing we do to excess, it is the dividing of the various capacities of man into watertight compartments. Certain things are sacred, certain things are secular, certain things may be done by the clergy and certain things may be done by politicians.' A very Australian attitude, but one that Menzies rejected, for 'one cannot separate life in that way and that you cannot separate what is sacred from what is secular; and that you cannot above all things have any Christianity which begins only on Sunday morning and ends on Sunday night'.[41]

He did not limit the sentiment to the parishioners. Speaking at the University of Adelaide ten years later, he advised that if we want to see a 'restoration of civilisation and peace', we need to see a restoration of the relationship between theory and prac-tice, between the 'skill of the hand and the wisdom of the mind', or, more loftily still, the 'spirit of humanity' or the 'human soul' and the 'human intellect'. Continuing with this thought, Menzies warned his audience that: 'It is worse than foolish, it is dangerous, to regard the spiritual nature of man as irrelevant to secular enterprise, or to treat a broad philosophy of life as an intellec-tual matter fit only for the university classroom.' The problems of the twentieth century were mere symptoms of our modern tendency 'to divide our lives into watertight compartments'.[42] In fact, Menzies expressed the same view nearly forty years earlier while a student himself, albeit in a more philosophical tone.[43]

Spirit and democracy

For Menzies, there was something sacred about democracy itself; like some dynamic divine will, it was a guide for a nation towards progress. Widely read democratic theorists of the time such as the Scottish–English philosopher A.D. Lindsay or the Catholic philosopher Jacques Maritain had not forgotten the historical connection between modern democracy and Christianity, puritan Christianity in particular in the case of Lindsay. As the Australian idealist Eggleston said in the midst of World War II, 'Christian ideas are the intellectual basis of nearly all social advance towards the emergence of personality. Moreover, most of the fighting towards this end has been done by the Christian.'[44] For many cultural commentators and public intellectuals before the mid-twentieth century, democracy in particular was an expression of the Christian ideal of all human beings bearing the *imago Dei* equally.[45] 'Surely it is not a mere accident,' Menzies said in the mid-1930s, 'that the era of democracy has given to us a new conception of human rights, of the dignity of labor, of standards of living and of health.'[46]

Democracy in England was set in motion by the Reform Act of 1832, which widened the franchise to include significant portions of the middle class. As a result of this act, said Menzies, 'the whole face of life has changed'. Working conditions have improved demonstrably; public sanitation has leaped ahead; and 'all the habits and mechanics of life have been revolutionised by a burst of inventive genius'. All of this is attributable, according to Menzies, to 'the new standing accord to man when he began to

find himself the master of his own political and social destiny'.[47]
Yet, as Menzies repeatedly said, democracy is not to be conceptualised in terms of machinery but rather in terms of spirit, and
when the spirit becomes weak, democracy becomes sick.

For Menzies, 'the great problem of self-government is not
historical or mechanical, but ethical'.[48] What Menzies called the
'sickness of democracy' was essentially short-sightedness, selfishness from citizens, and cowardice and opportunism from politicians
responding to the dynamics of electoral politics. He expressed the
problem with more cogency as Prime Minister in 1954:

> Demagogy is a poor substitute for democracy. Attempts to
> create 'class' hatred in a nation whose only true classes are
> the active and the idle are in truth attacks upon democracy.
> A vehement concentration upon 'rights' obscures the vital
> fact that unless duties are accepted and performed by each
> of us, not only our rights but the rights of others will die for
> want of nourishment. If we were all tired democrats, eager
> beneficiaries but reluctant contributors, democracy would
> collapse under its own weight.[49]

Menzies rephrased the thought: 'In a civilised community, not
one of us can live to himself. In the immortal phrase of St Paul,
"we are members one of another."'[50] Menzies' preservative against
the corruption of the democratic polity was elitist, with a Burkean
inflection. The problems of Australia during and after the war
must be solved by experts who are prepared to do hard thinking,
'not by a jury of men in the street but by the very best brains
and courage that this country can select'.[51] For Australians to
enjoy the advantage of Burkean statesmen, that is, politicians who
bring their '"matured judgement" to the service of the electors',[52]
the country must be producing individuals who are not merely

clever but also educated and wise. Or, in other words, citizens of spirit.

Next to atheistic communism and the apathy that goes with material prosperity, Menzies, like idealist philosophers in general,[53] warned Australians often about scientific materialism, or the view that a scientific education was sufficient to solve the problems facing civilisation. Unfortunately for the twentieth century, 'the spirit of man has not progressed with the skill of his hands', he wrote. Menzies thought that the spirit of man's 'greatest challenge in its history' was the 'disfiguring materialism' of the age.[54] Humans had to become loosed from materialism, for 'There can be no new social order worth while except on the basis of justice'.

> And justice is an affair of the spirit. It may prosaically and necessarily express itself in terms of the material things of life, but it will never be achieved by those who think only of those things. Man, ingenious man, mechanical man, has devised his machine and his systems and has become their slave. The real task in front of him is to become their master. For the Spirit must win![55]

But where was spirit to be found? Menzies' answer revealed the true Enlightenment man that he was. Salvation was to be found in education; an education system that was open to science and technology but resisted the corrosive effects of scientism and commericalism. In particular, Menzies turned to the institution that had been the keeper of the human spirit for centuries, the university.

Menzies' faith in the role of the university also revealed how much his world view had absorbed an English—even a liberal Anglican—understanding of the nature of government and of the need for a secular equivalent of the church for a polity to function properly. In this regard, it is worth remebering that Coleridge did not understand the church as a purely Christian institution but as a sort of estate of the realm.[56] It can be argued that Menzies brought together the democratic heritage that he had inherited from his Scottish background with the aristocratic ethos of the English, whom he so much admired.

The university for Menzies was the English church in the setting of an overseas British community that did not have an established church. It would correct the excesses of a modern commercial society and produce those people who would defend and protect the public good. In 'secular' Australia, only universities could play that role as national institutions that could rise above sordid particular interests.

Unlike modern libertarians, Menzies was not wholly suspicious of the power of government or the state. He believed that government had a positive role to play in ensuring the common good of the country. This was equally true of his understanding of the place of the universities in the wider scheme of things. Menzies did not view universities as adverserial institutions that would be at odds with the status quo. Rather they were to be seen as cooperating with other institutions; the vision was organic, deriving as it did from its idealist origins. Menzies was influenced by Smuts, and it was Smuts who coined the term Holism. The whole point of evolution, be it at a community level, a national level or an international level, was to replace conflict by cooperation. Human beings should work together, not be at each other's throats. That was the ideal of the commonwealth. The role of the university for Menzies was as an agent ensuring that this ideal would become reality.

5

EDUCATING FOR SPIRIT

The broad problem, of which all these matters that I have
mentioned are merely aspects, is the problem of education for
citizenship ... The greatest failure in the world in my lifetime ...
has not been the failure in mechanical capacity or manual capacity
half as much as it has been the failure of the human spirit.
Speech by the Rt Hon R.G. Menzies KC, MP on Education,
30 July 1945

There are two key periods in the history of the government's role
in the development of education in Australia. The first ranges
from the early 1860s to the early 1880s and was concerned with
the establishment of a system of state schools at an elementary,
or primary, level in each of the colonies.[1] Schools were to be run
by the state, attendance compulsory and the instruction secular, although what was meant by 'secular' varied from colony to
colony.[2] Most importantly, state funding was withdrawn from
all denominational schools, which meant that those denomina-
tions that sought to provide an education that included religion
had to find the means to support those schools. In particular this
meant the Catholic Church, which refused to countenance secular

education as it was defined in state schools. They were aided in their efforts by a large number of vocations by young men and especially young women, who joined the various teaching orders, thereby making the Catholic school system viable. A Herculean feat maintained for around a hundred years.

It can be said that the creation of a set of state schools in each of the colonies was one of the great achievements of colonial Australia, matched only by the building of the railways in each colony. The establishment of a school system was one of the first major administrative achievements of Australia. The one great failing was its inability to accommodate Catholic Australians. If the periods from the 1860s to the 1880s was the first heroic age of Australian education, it must be said that the 1950s and 1960s was the second.[3] If it was Henry Parkes who placed his stamp on the first period, it was Sir Robert Menzies who did the same for the second.

When Menzies re-established the Liberal Party in 1944, he was also, in a real sense, re-establishing liberalism in Australia. Of greatest significance is the fact that he was doing so at the national level. The key issue is what sort of liberalism and, more importantly, what sort of individual did he have in mind? Two things stand out. The first is that Menzies' liberalism and his understanding of the individual had been informed not only by cultural puritanism but also by philosophical idealism—itself shaped by the cultural puritanism of the nineteenth century. His ideal individual combined a sense of independence with a strong notion of duty and responsibility.

The second is that Menzies' liberalism was closely tied to his educational ideals and his understanding that education was a primary means through which an individual developed his or her individuality, or personality. Menzies published a considerable amount of material on education, as well as delivering many speeches on the topic across the whole of his political career. He had what might be described as a well-developed philosophy of education that had strong roots in the idealist intellectual milieu of his formative years in Melbourne.

Menzies' liberalism was closely tied to his views on education and the belief that education was a means of ensuring that human beings progressed and developed and were able to transcend their failings and weaknesses. Material progress by itself, argued Menzies on a number of occasions, can lead to barbarism and all the terrible events of the twentieth century. It needed to be complemented by some sort of moral and spiritual progress, and a key factor in that progress was to be a humanities education. Menzies was perfectly aware of the human capacity to perform evil acts, but, as a good liberal, he did not subscribe to the idea of a fallen human nature that could not be saved without the (unearned) gift of God's grace. In this regard he stood with David Hume and the Scottish Anglophiles of the Scottish Enlightenment, not the dour and miserable Calvinists. Menzies was essentially an optimist, unlike the pessimistic atheist Calvinist John Anderson, who stood in opposition to the whole basis of Menzies' education philosophy.

John Anderson was not a product of Australian education, but was formed in the wide-ranging system of his native Scotland, with its austere Calvinist demand for system, depth, breadth and rigour.[4] Whereas the conservative ideal of the university followed Newman and Matthew Arnold, emphasising truth and culture as the end of the university, Anderson emphasised critique: 'The work of the academic, *qua* academic, is criticism; and whatever his special field may be, his development of independent views will bring him into conflict with prevailing opinions and customary attitudes in the public arena and not merely among his fellow professionals.'[5] Anderson had his exemplar:

Socrates did not deny, but rather gloried in the fact, that he had striven by example and precept to inculcate the spirit of criticism, to encourage the questioning of received opinions and traditions ... The Socratic education begins, then, with the awakening of the mind to the need for criticism, to the uncertainty of the principles by which is supposed itself to be guided.[6]

In describing Socrates, Anderson was, of course, describing himself. Anderson found himself fighting a difficult battle against both political conservatism—the young Anderson had been a communist—and moral conservatism—Anderson was also a sexual libertine. Anderson himself went through a profound change and, like Menzies, came to see the spirit of science as the greatest threat to the preservation of culture and excellence. This and the oppressive tendencies of Marxism, which Anderson eventually abandoned, would lead Anderson to emphasise culture or 'classicism' as the standard of critique.

Anderson himself underwent a conversion, albeit a gradual one, from communism to an anti-communism that valued classicism in the university. In any event, Anderson's emphasis on critique was never slavishly Marxist, which enabled him eventually to turn against communism itself and become something of an elite cultural conservative, seeing the university as a crucial preservative against the tendency of the sciences—themselves strongly linked to utility—to declare all disciplines deemed unscientific as arbitrary, obscurantist and indulgent. In some ways Anderson's view of the university turned out to be not so different from Menzies'. In the end, according to Anderson, it was the hegemonic status of the sciences that fatally wounded the university. By 1960 he could lament that 'neither the notion of culture nor the classical outlook is now accorded any great respect even in reputedly educated circles'.[7] The emphasis on critique survived Anderson but became divided between the Andersonians and the neo-Marxists, the latter coming to dominate humanities faculties from the 1960s, eventually morphing into the postmodernists from the late 1980s.

Menzies' educational philosophy was within a tradition of thinking about the university that competed with other 'ideas of a university' throughout Australian history.[8] The first professor appointed to Sydney University, John Woolley,[9] described a 'liberal education' as 'one which cultivates and develops in their due and harmonious proportion what the Romans called "humanitas", all those faculties and powers which distinguish man from the inferior creatures'.[10] Like Woolley, Menzies defined his vision of education against utilitarianism, sharing Woolley's sweetness-and-light vision of the purpose of a university. Its purpose was the preservation of culture and civilisation defined in cultural humanist terms.

Menzies' idea of a university

Menzies was the first Australian prime minister after Deakin to be the product of an Australian university. As pointed out earlier, both Deakin and Menzies imbibed a Melburnian intellectual milieu steeped in idealism. Just a couple of years before his 'Forgotton People' radio talks, Menzies had reflected at length on the nature of the university and its salutary relationship to civilisation. On 26 April 1939 Menzies gave a speech entitled 'The place of a university in the modern community'. The speech was to commemorate the tenth year of Canberra University College. It would not be until 3 September 1939 that Menzies would fulfil his melancholy duty of telling Australians that they were British allies at war with Germany. But the world knew that war was coming, and Menzies told his audience that 'old beliefs are being challenged and old values reassessed'; that 'barbaric philosophies of blood and iron are resurgent'.[11]

Warfare was indeed a threat to civilisation. But if civilisation was most embodied in the university, then, for Menzies, there was a more insidious threat that had emerged in recent times: materialism in all its meanings. 'We have commercialised most things; we have fallen down and worshipped idols of gold and silver and brass, most of them with clay feet.'[12] The university must be a home of 'pure culture and learning', but how can it stand against the pragmatic materialism brought about by the world of commerce? 'The world is full of "practical" men. Their philosophy is utilitarian. They have weighed the classics, literature and philosophy in their commercial balances and found them wanting because unprofitable. They have put pure learning on the defensive.'[13]

What Menzies called 'utilitarianism' could never be the foundation of a civilisation; it was a 'Frankenstein monster which may yet destroy us'. How? Because our civilisation has become 'preoccupied with means rather than ends'; with speed and efficiency, rather than quality leisure time in which we can pursue learning and culture. But as long as the age is utilitarian this is to be expected, for that philosophy ignores the 'humane and imperishable elements in man'; indeed, 'the mere mechanics of life can never be the sole vocation of the human spirit'.[14]

A humanities education would ensure that democracy in Australia remained on the straight and narrow and was not corrupted by the possible vices that material progress could encourage. It would perform the following tasks:

- create good democratic citizens who would not be trapped by their narrow provincial concerns
- ensure that material progress did not again lead to barbarism of the sort that had already scarred the twentieth century
- provide the appropriate elite leadership required by a democracy, a leadership that would be marked by intelligence and moral responsibility.

It can be argued that after World War II Australia rededi-
cated itself to progress, in a similar fashion to the Australia of
the 1860s and 1870s, which had inaugurated the first educational
revolution.[15] It was Menzies' great achievement to provide an
updated liberal understanding of what progress meant in contrast
to the social democratic vision provided by his Labor opponents.
Australia would become a country engaged in secondary manufacturing industry, which required an educated population and a
scientific infrastructure. This entailed expanding both secondary
education and the universities.

This idea of progress as national development established
itself firmly as the core public philosophy of Australia. It was
Menzies' role to ensure that this ideal was rooted in his particular
tradition of liberalism and not socialism, and that it moved in the
direction of civilisation, not barbarism. The corruption of the university will therefore corrupt our democracy, for the university
is a crucial character-forming institution for leaders, and it takes
character to stand against the tide of populism and civil vice that
always threatens a democracy. Citing Edmund Burke ('that fount
of clear thinking and resolve'[16]), Menzies idealised the statesman
who offered the people 'not only their votes but their character
and their judgement'.[17]

A belief in the power of education to effect progress has been
a crucial element of liberalism since the nineteenth century in
Australia. It rests on a faith that, just as it is possible to improve
the material conditions of humanity, so human beings can also be
improved in a moral, intellectual and spiritual manner. As we have
already shown, late nineteenth-century liberalism in Australia, as
in other parts of the English-speaking world, had come to possess
strong links with philosophical idealism and its belief in the development of 'personality' as the product of the evolution of both
the individual and the collective. In Australia the most coherent

expression of this philosophical liberalism was F.W. Eggleston's *Search for a Social Philosophy* published in 1941.

Menzies was clearly influenced by idealism and did occasionally invoke the idea of personality. For Menzies, as for most liberals, the power of education lay in its capacity to improve individuals, thereby allowing them to be the motor of social progress. Education gave individuals the capacity to bring a better world into being. Moreover, for idealist liberals, progress would lead to the creation of a world in which autonomous individuals would develop a strong sense of social cooperation, thereby enabling them to work together willingly for the common good. Eggleston referred to this as the 'Christian ethic'.[18] The goal was an integrated cooperative society in which all elements of the social order worked together in harmony. The underlying ideal, found for example in Elton Mayo[19] and profoundly Christian in its origins, was that of the human body in which all the parts worked together.[20] Harmony, not conflict, was the desired outcome. Hence, the goal of liberal education was to produce men and women who were willing to serve the state, thereby enhancing the common good. This was an older nineteenth-century ideal, advocated by such academics as Charles Badham, and its outcome was the extraordinary generation of men who drew up the Commonwealth Constitution and ran the early Commonwealth.

Menzies was an enthusiastic advocate of education as an essential liberal element of any attempt to create a progressive Australia founded on the energy and activities of its individual citizens. The humanities were central to this vision. But that did not mean that he wanted to rush out and use the power of the Commonwealth Government to impose his educational vision on the country. Menzies was a constitutionalist and was well aware of the value of the separation of powers, quoting Montesquieu in support of that principle: 'Montesquieu, who had such an influence upon organic political science, had no respect for uniformity. He looked for a system (which the United States and Australia to a degree adopted) where there is a division of power, where power checks power.'[21]

Nor at any stage did he seek to intervene in curriculum matters. Menzies did not express any direct interest in what schools and universities should teach. In fact he deliberately stayed out of such matters on the assumption—naively, in hindsight—that educational institutions knew how to behave properly.[22] Funding was Menzies' primary interest.

Menzies' understanding of the humanities tended to be somewhat vague. He did not seek to revive the classics, perhaps because, unlike his mentor Owen Dixon, he appears not to have been an enthusiastic classicist; at university he needed two attempts to pass Latin I.[23] Although his speeches indicate the way in which the Bible had formed the 'furniture of his mind', there is little indication that he had much in the way of knowledge of the classical world or classical authors. His view of the humanities seems to have been coloured by his idealism and its accompanying ideals of a vague spirituality and citizenship as well as by his understanding of what it meant to be British. Menzies' conception of the humanities was founded largely on a combination of his love for English literature and a somewhat woolly idealism; it stood at the opposite extreme to John Anderson's tough-minded view of classicism as relentless criticism. Menzies stood for all those notions of democracy, the state, citizenship and the universities that Anderson spent his career criticising.

The most important issue for understanding Menzies and the actions that his government took in relation to education is the connection between his philosophy of education and the policies that were adopted. In the twenty-first century it is too often assumed that Commonwealth involvement in educational matters, both universities and schools, was both inevitable and something positive. But Canada, for obvious reasons, does not have a federal department of education. Menzies believed in both progress and the efficacy of education as a motor of progress, but that did not mean that this would automatically translate into Commonwealth money to support education. A liberalism based on idealism and with a considerable emphasis on education emphasises a quite different type of individual to one that focuses on entrepreneurial and business activity. Liberal idealism was attractive to professionals as it emphasised duty and cooperation. It remained the dominant form of philosophy in Australia until after World War II with the one exception of the Sydney Andersonians.

Menzies believed that the government of the day, the public service and the universities should work together and that, in an ideal world, the public service would be run by people who had received a liberal education at university. Menzies understood this as the English model. Government and the universities will work together. There can be little doubt that Menzies sought to create an elite that would be intelligent, with an enlarged moral sense, who would ensure that Australia was well governed. It would be an elite based on merit, an expression of the ideals of aristocratic liberalism, in which the best had authority. Menzies was undoubtedly a democrat, although he also recognised the need for a democracy to produce educated leaders who possessed a broad vision.

What Menzies did not appreciate was that the intellectual elite on which he pinned so much hope was turning adversarial and rationalist. It increasingly wanted to oppose the government, not to work with it. As idealism was supplanted in Australia, so was the older idea of an ideal of social harmony replaced by an emphasis on conflict as being central to the way in which the social order worked. Menzies may have regarded his fellow Australian politicians as a collection of Lilliputians, but he failed to appreciate that university education was less likely to lead to agreement than spawning intellectual quarrels regarding the best end to open an egg.

Menzies also failed to appreciate the magnitude of changes taking place in the ideological atmosphere of the universities. Certainly in the mid-1950s the political and moral conservatism of the universities was strong enough to end the career of University of Tasmania philosopher Sydney Orr and play a part in Russel Ward's failure to obtain a position at the University of New South Wales.[24] Ten years later when the appointment of Frank Knopfelmacher—a prominent anti-communist—was overturned by the Sydney University Senate, accusations of leftist domination of the university started to fly.[25] Even if the Knopfelmacher case was ambiguous in terms of whether the withdrawal of the professorship was ideological or due to Knopfelmacher's alleged uncollegial personality, it was around this time that conservative academics were noticing a far more assertive and dominant leftism in the humanities departments. Marxists were taking over, and their Baby-Boomer students would finish the job of transforming universities from conservers of culture to deconstructors of culture. Like his ideal of a British Australia, Menzies' ideal of the university as a place of cultural enhancement and the pursuit of truth, beauty and goodness was becoming untenable not long after he retired in 1966.

Donald Horne's observations, published in 1964, of 'the academic' are telling in terms of a transition that was taking place in the universities:

Before the Second World War the general line of belief of the most influential Australian academics was, on the whole, conservative ... There is still some of this conservatism left, although it is necessarily changed in style, but on the whole Australian academics now hold orthodox Australian liberal opinions: they are critical of censorship, licensing laws, hanging and the police; *in politics they would tend to distrust the Liberal Party, hate the Democratic Labor Party and despair of the Labor Party ...*[26]

For Horne, the average academic, if not yet a radical, was certainly left-leaning. Their students would become radicalised during the late 1960s and throughout the early to mid-1970s, mainly owing to the Vietnam War and the incredible opportunity it provided for Marxist critique to seize the imagination of the middle-class educated youth (not to mention international celebrities like Jane Fonda and John Lennon). In fact, Horne's full discussion of the academic and the university in his *Lucky Country* still largely rings true today and repays rereading. In all the present conservative talk of leftist ideology destroying the universities, we must bear in mind that one of the great agents of cultural destruction was in fact the rapid vocationalisation and bureaucratisation of the universities after World War II and again from the late 1980s with the neoliberal Dawkins reforms under the Labor Party.[27] As the Menzies-initiated funding was withdrawn, university bureaucracies exploded, partly because of the logic of bureaucracy itself and partly because bureaucracy was required to find new sources of income and to work full-time meeting the requirements of the highly conditional public funding that was available.

As has been argued, Menzies was an Anglophile Australian of Scottish descent who idealised what he saw as 'Englishness' as a set of cultural attributes. This can be seen clearly in his essay on 'The English tradition':

The travelling Englishman, the writing Englishman, the politically vocal Englishman, the governing Englishman in scattered colonies and protectorates has, so far, been broadly the educated Englishman. Education in England has a long and, if you like, conservative tradition behind it. The educated Englishman, therefore, has certain inherited and acquired mental habits which deserve study. He cannot be explained in a sentence, or disposed of by a single epigram. He is probably the most civilized of human beings; he is certainly one of the most complex.[28]

It would not be unfair to say that Menzies was very much concerned with the 'educated Australian' and the possible means of creating a collection of such individuals who would become the leadership group of a democratic society. Menzies was an aristocratic liberal who understood that if democracy was to grow and prosper it required to be led by an educated elite who were devoted to the public good and who ruled on behalf of those who had elected them. Note the following comment from *The Forgotten People*: 'To discourage ambition, to envy success, to have achieved superiority, to distrust independent thought, to sneer at and impute false motives to public service—these are the maladies of modern democracy and of Australian democracy in particular.'[29]

A healthy democracy would appreciate and make good use of the ambitions of those who sought recognition and who entered public service to benefit the public good. A harmony between the ambitious few and the democratic citizenry was to be central to democracy. Hence during his career Menzies' educational focus was primarily on the Australian university because it embodied what was best about England and the English, an institution that would produce the educated leaders of the future.

Menzies clearly believed that an organic relationship should exist between the university and the society of which it was part. The contemplative life of the university enriches the soul but, for Menzies, the active life is to be preferred over the contemplative one. Perhaps the most important aspect of Menzies' comments are those on leadership, which indicates the way in which he understood the relationship between the educated leaders and the rest in a democracy: 'Democracy demands leaders and leadership. It demands leaders who will not be afraid to tell the people that they are wrong and to persuade and guide them. I do not deny, on the contrary I uphold, the right of the people to censure freely, to criticize, to elect, to reject.'[30]

Menzies' view of the relationship between the university and the wider society in a democracy is a classical expression of aristocratic liberalism. There is an assumption underpinning it that independent individuals who follow their ambition and take up the mantle of leadership will somehow have a harmony of interests with those who they lead.

There is a consistency in Menzies' writings on education across the decades from the 1930s to the 1960s with a focus on the need for a balance between material advancement and the ethical and the spiritual, the need to create good citizens and the problems of leadership in a democratic society. In a major speech on education delivered in the House of Representatives in 1945, Menzies stated the following:

The broad problem, of which all these matters that I have mentioned are merely aspects, is the problem of education for citizenship ... The greatest failure in the world in my lifetime ... has not been the failure in mechanical capacity or manual capacity half as much as it has been the failure of the human spirit. War after war is the result of a failure of the human spirit, not of some superficial elements but of the fatal instability of man to adjust himself to other men in a social world. With all of our scientific development of this century, it still remains true that 'the proper study of man is man' and that the real 'peace-maker' is human understanding. The closer the countries of the world have come to each other in point of time, the more they have tended, unhappily, to develop a narrow spirit of self-sufficiency. The more absorbed the people become in the technique of material living, the more they have neglected their moral responsibilities and the more, unhappily, they have neglected the problems of popular government.[31]

Now consider this extract from a radio broadcast Menzies made in 1954:

But what do we mean by education? I have known men with University degrees who remained basically stupid and unperceptive and selfish. I have known men who had no schooling after they were thirteen, who spoke what we would call bad English, but who had character, wisdom, reflection and a warm understanding of their fellow-men.

Education does not simply mean the compulsory getting of a stock of knowledge. Knowledge is good; but wisdom is better. It is the way a man's mind works that matters. To be educated is to have learned how to think; to have acquired self-discipline; to have understood duty and the rights of others.

These tasks are not merely scientific or mechanical. A man may be a great scientist and be uncivilised. He may have mastered the technique of the law but have no real understanding of its spirit. Education must produce a sense of values, high ethical standards and a spirit of tolerance, or it fails.[32]

Finally this paper, delivered to the 1961 conference 'The Challenges to Australian Education', in which Menzies provides his definition of the purpose of education: 'Once we get above the rudiments, education is the business, I repeat, of producing an educated personality. The work of organising a community educational service is therefore a complex one, requiring great skill, devotion and understanding. What is to be aimed at is a general system, producing individuals of great variety.'[33]

Education in Australia, he argued, has two great tasks. First there is the need 'to train as many students as possible in bodies of knowledge which will make them more competent to deal with the practical affairs of life. We must train and equip more competent workers in every branch of every industry; more and better scientists and technologists, more and better administrators, engineers, doctors and lawyers.'[34] But, as shown in chapter 4, Menzies is fully aware of both the limitations of modern science and the need to find a remedy to the human propensity for evil.

At its core stood the need to produce an 'educated personality' who would be a good citizen, a desire to embrace science as part of the basis of modern progress and the need for proper moral development so that human beings will be able to keep up with the advancement of science and the relevance of education for democracy. It is a liberal vision of progress. The horrors of the first half of the twentieth century were no doubt at the back Menzies' mind. He was determined that liberal progress was not only desirable but also, in the face of human weakness, an achievable goal. Nor was he alone in his task of creating an educated personality. Consider this quote from James Darling, the headmaster of Geelong Grammar: 'The civilised man, sensitive, wide in his interests, tolerant and yet courageous, intellectual and strong in principle, is our ideal and it is by our education that we must pursue it.'[35]

Menzies' critique of utilitarian materialism also had implications for the system of primary and high school education in Australia, which he frequently described as 'purely secular'.

Menzies' support of denominational schools and an expanded university system were closely bound up with his more comprehensive diagnosis of the twentieth century as an age of destructive materialism. As early as 1943 he was openly concerned about the future survival of denominational schools in what he predicted would be lean economic years after the war. Menzies sympathised with parents who paid high school fees to secure a denominational education for their children yet were also forced to pay taxes for public schools to which they could not in good conscience send their children. Why should such schools not receive state funding? Menzies consistently held that religion was a valuable component of education, and its absence from what he called the 'purely secular' public system was a great cause for concern. This was a major reason why he thought state aid to denominational schools was justified.[36]

Menzies' education policy

Menzies' decision to offer state aid was not merely because he thought the existing system unjust. For Menzies, religion was a crucial preservative of the spirit of man that he saw rapidly eroding. In a remarkable speech delivered to the Commonwealth Parliament in 1945, Menzies affirmed that Australia would need to expand its scientific and technical traning to compete with an increasingly global economy. If Australian grains were going to compete with grains produced more cheaply by other countries, Australia would have to figure out how to grow them more efficiently and cheaply. In Menzies' own words, 'We must begin, not to follow the world, but to lead it in technical skill.'[37] In other words, a comprehensive expansion of the sciences in education was unavoidable in the emerging global economy. But this was fraught with danger. 'The greatest failure in the world in my lifetime', Menzies told the Commonwealth Parliament, 'has not been the failure in technical capacity or manual capacity half as much as it has been the failure of the human spirit.'[38] This failure of the spirit was very much a public issue, for it weakened the bonds of society and therefore the strength of Australian democracy: 'The more absorbed the people become in technical and material living, the more they have neglected their social responsibilities and the more, unhappily, they have neglected the problems of popular self-government. It is well to remember that for years, the greatest danger to democracy has been, not so much a danger from without, as a danger from within.'[39]

He stated it well in a 1947 *New York Times* piece in which he described the history of the twentieth century as 'a tragic story of how science ... has outrun the art of living, to the singular discomfort and confusion and almost to the ruin of mankind'.[40] Or, again, when he said that 'the subtlest of all attacks on freedom is the one which comes from within'.[41] Quoting General Smuts and echoing the influential social analysis of Hilaire Belloc, he warned that when citizens 'abdicate the responsibility of judgement in favour of somebody else',[42] over time they become 'servile'.[43] Menzies went on in his speech to parliament to praise the British Education Act of 1944, which, he was happy to say, 'imposes on local education authorities a duty to contribute towards "the spiritual, moral, mental and physical development of the community"'. This entailed a duty to begin each school day with 'collective worship', as well as teaching non-sectarian religion within normal school hours, with appropriate exemptions.[44]

Menzies also diagnosed the problem as a symptom of the decline of the 'classical notion of education' in terms of the endeavour 'to produce a good man and a good citizen', something particularly chronic in Australia, with Australians' characteristic impatience for 'useless learning' and tendency to demand 'that our sons and daughters shall be taught things at school which will enable them to earn money after they have left school and nothing else'.[45] If religion teaches sacred duties between citizen and citizen, a classical education enables citizens to 'become aware of the problems of the world' and to acquire 'some quality of intellectual criticism' yet with 'detachment of judgement' and 'always to moderate passion and prejudice'.[46]

Indeed, in Menzies' first term as Prime Minister with the Liberal Party from 1949, he began a slow and piecemeal program of state funding for denominational schools and university colleges. In 1952 his government amended existing laws to allow tax deductions of private school fees for up to £50 per year. Although the amount was small, it would be increased over time. Over the following years there would be further changes allowing tax deductions for private donations for denominational school buildings (1954). Also in 1964, £5 million was set aside for the provision of science buildings and equipment for all secondary schools, public or denominational. And, in 1964, 10 000 new government scholarships became available to all secondary school children, in both the public and the denominational systems.[47]

Throughout this period Menzies continued to warn Australians of the dangers of materialism and to encourage religion and education as the preservative of human spirit. On the eve of the Space Race Menzies continued to warn Australians of the limitations of science for addressing a social malaise that he detected: 'Let us by all means have scientists and the best we can find. But let us also have people of humane letters, who can remind us that the most important thing in the world is not the machine, but man.'[48] For Menzies, the materialism that puts its trust solely in science and technology, with no religion, begets only crisis:

> The most important thing in the world, may I say for myself, is man's relation to his maker: his relation to the divine and

spiritual law. The second most important thing is man's relation to man, with all that it implies of brotherhood and understanding and fair play and responsibility. The third is man's scientific and mechanical skill and the extension of the boundaries of knowledge. To this third one the 20th century has devoted most of its genius with results sometimes magnificent, as in medicine and industrial production and transport and living standards; and sometimes disastrous, as in the mass destruction of modern war. But it cannot truly be said that the 20th century is the century of true religion; for in sheer paganism we have occasionally put the Dark Ages to shame. Nor can it be said that humanity has got to know itself and its duties better, for international hatreds have seldom been more acute.[49]

As usual, Menzies went on to prescribe education as the only answer, but not merely a technical or scientific education, for 'To be educated is to have learned how to think; to have acquired self-discipline; to have understood duty and the rights of others'. Furthermore, 'These tasks are not merely scientific or mechanical'.[50] He said in another speech that 'we must reassert the truth, that materialism is not enough. Man does not live by bread alone.' Indeed, 'slavery to the gods of material well-being is a degrading slavery'. Yet we hold the remedy within the hands of our own heritage, for 'we have inherited great spiritual traditions of unselfish service'.[51] Again, education was the answer, but we must beware of the current 'contempt for the humanities' or so-called 'non-utilitarian studies'. For it is 'that spiritual enlightenment which alone can bring a man to his full growth'.[52]

It was the comprehensive vision of the decline of spirit with the rise of materialism outlined above that lay behind the remarks made by Menzies in his introduction to the important 1957

Murray Report on Australian universities,[53] which heralded the new age of university expansion and government patronage. As Menzies reminded the architects of the modern Australian university, '[C]ivilisation in the true sense requires a close and growing attention not only to science in all its branches, but also to those studies of the mind and spirit of man, of history, of literature and language and mental and moral philosophy … the relative neglect of which has left a gruesome mark on this century.' In short, 'Let us have more scientists and more humanists', or, better still, 'Let the scientists be touched and informed by the humanists … [and] the humanists touched and informed by science'.[54] All of this was necessary if 'we are to raise our spiritual, intellectual and material living standards'.[55] With a rising global population, not to mention a post-war population boom in Australia, there would be greater strain on resources, requiring a greater emphasis on science for the purpose of increasing production and efficiency. But Menzies' great fear was of an education system without ethics, science without humanity, 'means without ends'. Such a system was deeply inhuman:

> I use the word *ethics* in a general way; not as denoting 'Christian ethics', though to many of us these are the highest; not in any discriminating sense. Christianity remains, as a Scottish preacher once said, dramatically in my hearing, 'the greatest minority movement in the history of the world'. But there are other religions with their own ethical rules and moral compulsions. The main thing is that education must not be so resolutely utilitarian as to be pagan and degrading. Secular education must not come to mean selfish education.[56]

Menzies continued: 'I have stressed the point of ethics because I believe that the most important thing to consider and learn in this world is the nature of man, his duties and rights, his place in society, his relationship to his Creator.'[57]

Menzies delivered the final blow to materialistic approaches to social progress. Science was simply not enough to save civilisation from materialistic selfishness:

> It is a common, but attractive error, [sic] to think of modern advances in applied science, from the telephone to television, from the motor-car to aircraft to rockets and space vehicles, as in themselves the proof of advancing civilisation. These are among the mere mechanical aids to civilisation. They may be wisely or wickedly used. Civilisation is in the hearts and minds of men. It will advance or fall back according to the use we make of knowledge and of skill. In spite of all we have had to our hands, the twentieth century has seen more of greed and of inhumanity, more of war and barbarism, more of hatred and envy and malice, than any of us could have foreseen when we were young and hopeful. We have seen great skill employed with hatred; science with envy; diplomacy with threat and blackmail; the distraction, as I personally believe, of too many skilled people from improving the lot of mankind upon earth to a tremendous competition in space, in which prestige threatens to out-match usefulness. We must recapture our desire to know more and feel more, about our fellowmen [sic]; to have a philosophy of living; to elevate the dignity of man, a dignity which, in our Christian concept, arises from our belief that he is made in the image of his Maker.[58]

The following year, in a speech before the Australasian Medical Congress, Menzies described Soviet Russia as 'an administration which is purely materialist in philosophy'.[59] Yet such materialism was not unique to Russia. Indeed, it is preference for the material over the spiritual, or, as Menzies sometimes rendered it, 'this confusing of means with ends that has bedevilled the twentieth century'.[60] It had thus far been a century 'disfigured' by 'widespread attacks upon the religion of love by organised hatreds and cruelties of the most barbarous kind'.[61] Whether science achieves good or ill for humanity 'will depend upon the minds and spirits of those who use the instrument'. Crucially for his argument, Menzies pointed out that 'science and wisdom have no necessary connection'.[62] He went on: 'If we look at the matter in this way, we see science in its proper perspective; not as the master, but as the servant. We are not to adapt the Shorter Catechism to read "The chief end of men is to glorify science and enjoy it forever."'[63]

To return to the practical dimension of Menzies' vision of education, the only problem, of course, was that education was not a Commonwealth matter and Menzies was a good constitutionalist. There was little he could do in the education realm unless opportunities presented themselves to him. In this regard, the key factor seems to have been the inability, or unwillingness, of the states to fund their increasing education needs at a time when financial power was moving towards the Commonwealth. The old education order was the creation of the first education revolution of the nineteenth century. It had seen only a fraction of students complete much in the way of secondary education and an even smaller fraction attend university. Moreover, the states did not have the burden of educating that significant proportion of students who attended Catholic and other private schools. Older-style teaching methods allowed for large classes, and the amount of technology required was not high. Nevertheless educational standards at the elite high schools, both public and private, were quite high because they educated only students of a high calibre. Given Australia's occupational profile, there was little need, or desire, to expand the education system significantly. Moreover the 1930s saw a decline in the birth rate.

This had begun to change by the late 1940s with an increase in the birth rate and an enlarged immigrant intake. The cost of education began to rise. To give an example, although there was a small decline in the number of secondary students in New South Wales between 1945 and 1950, between 1950 and 1960 the number of secondary schools and students doubled.[64] There was also a significant increase in the number of university students. Put simply, education had again become an important public policy issue in Australia, just as it had been in the 1860s and 1870s.

What then did Australian universities look like during the 1950s?[65] The first thing to note is that they still regarded Britain, and in particular Oxbridge, as their spiritual home and source of inspiration. This was not surprising given that the 1950s was the last decade in which strong ties between Australia and Britain seemed to be natural to both parties. Australian universities were small provincial institutions that dreamed of Oxbridge but exhibited clearly that the Scottish universities had been their founding model. There was little interest in American education and even less in that of continental Europe. As P.H. Partridge pointed out in the early 1950s, there was an attitude in the wider Australian community that the universities themselves were to blame for some of their problems.[66] It can be argued that they had not put down deep roots in their communities and were regarded as somewhat exotic institutions, a view that went back to the nineteenth century. They trained professionals and teachers, but they were not regarded with enormous affection by large numbers of Australians. There appears to have been a disjuncture between universities' somewhat inflated and romantic view of themselves and the reality of university life in Australia. Menzies clearly shared that romantic view, along with an ideal of the humanities that had a powerful religious or spiritual dimension. But it could be said that Menzies hoped to make that ideal a reality.

Some Commonwealth funding for universities had commenced under Menzies' predecessor, but it is Menzies who took the major steps towards Commonwealth funding of universities when he accepted the recommendations of the Murray Report. There was a slow and elaborate courtship ritual between the Commonwealth and the universities, as represented by the Australian Vice-Chancellors' Committee (AVCC), before they embraced each other in what would become a very peculiar union.

Some of the features of that courtship are as follows: 'The universities and the AVCC clearly wanted funding from some source. The Commonwealth looked like the best bet as it had become financially dominant within the Australian system of government. The universities did not receive large amounts of money from bequests or from their alumni.'[67] According to the Murray Report, by the 1950s only 15.6 per cent of their income came from fees.[68]

The universities had expanded in the post-war period; they probably needed to expand physically. But, if that was the case, why was so little income being earned from fees? The universities launched a campaign emphasising how they were in crisis and in need of an injection of funds. Menzies did not move precipitously as he had other concerns and appears to have been wary of extending Commonwealth responsibilities. From 1951 onwards the Commonwealth had made some grants to the universities under Section 96 of the Constitution but they required that universities supply three times the grant from state governments and fees.[69]

Finally, in 1956, Menzies established the Murray Committee, or Committee on Australian Universities, which was composed of two British academics, the Australian head of the CSIRO who was a fervent advocate of Commonwealth funding for universities, and two senior businessmen. Surprisingly, there do not seem to have been any economists or financial experts on the panel, no one to ask how much this might cost in the longer term. This was a very British way of doing things; when higher education was expanded in Britain, it was done on the haziest of notions of economic growth (which turned out to be wrong) and with little consideration of how it was going to be funded. As Noel Annan points out, in Britain where the same Murray was in charge of universities as he who gave advice to the Commonwealth Government, '[T]he wave of expansion gathered such momentum that when it broke it left devastation behind it.'[70]

The Murray Committee, it could be said, let the children loose in the lolly shop. The lobby group was allowed to decide what should be done. Moreover, Menzies accepted the recommendations of the report.

Looking at the Murray Report, a number of things stand out:

- It is framed within a doctrine of national progress and development in which the growth of manufacturing industry is given prominence along with the idea that science is now crucial for any country wishing to prosper.
- The educational philosophy mirrored that of Menzies, with a humanistic rationale combined with arguments in favour of science. There was no real scrutiny of what the place of universities was or should be in Australia. No attempt was made to look beyond an accepted British ideal of a university. A certain model of the university was assumed. In particular, the report supported the idea of academic autonomy and of academics being left free to follow their inquiries wherever they might lead.
- There appears to have been no discussion regarding the issue of raising fees or of exploring other means of funding universities.

- It advocated a £500 p.a. increase for professors.[71] In 1955 the minimum annual pay for adult males was £764. In 2015 terms, that would be about $20 000 p.a.
- Treasury had been sidelined from the process, and there appear to have been no estimates of what Commonwealth funding for universities might entail in future decades.[72]

This was Menzies' great triumph; or was it? Certainly, historians who have written on the topic, such as Alan Martin and Cameron Hazlehurst, have tended to hail Menzies as the great saviour of Australian universities.[73] More recently, Hannah Forsyth has disagreed, seeing Menzies' funding of the universities as a Commonwealth grab for control, citing a 1959 cabinet document, which states: 'Money is the weapon by which oversight of universities will be secured.'[74] There is another possibility, which is that the AVCC hoodwinked Menzies into giving them what they wanted. The only problem with that interpretation is that, in appointing Murray as chair of the committee, Menzies seems to have been conniving at giving the universities what they sought.

In some ways, given who could afford to go to university in the 1950s, it looks suspiciously like a case of middle-class welfare. Why, for example, did Menzies not canvass the issue of increased fees for students? Surely, given the values that Menzies had espoused since the *Forgotten People* of the self-reliant individualism of the middle class, he should have supported some sort of increased contribution by those who received the benefits of such an education. Allan Martin suggests that the funding of the universities was motivated by a desire to counter the idea that the ALP was more friendly to universities and education than the Liberal Party.[75]

The major implication of the Murray Report was that the intervention by the Commonwealth completed the process whereby universities became rent seekers of the Australian taxpayer rather than independent entities. It also raised the spectre of increasing Commonwealth control of universities over time in terms of setting their priorities and directing what they would do. In the short term, the triumph of the universities as embodied by the implementation of the Murray Report served to increase academic hubris and perhaps to increase the distance separating the universities from the wider Australian community. As it seemed to confirm the 'aura' that universities placed around themselves, it encouraged academics to think that they had a 'special place', including a privileged right to criticism. Interestingly, Menzies made an observation on this matter in a speech delivered to the University of New South Wales in the course of which he defended free speech: 'Freedom is to be seen as a faculty enjoyed by all citizens, not because they are academic or because they conduct a newspaper, but because they are citizens.'[76]

Of course, in all of this one has to recognise that the Australian tradition of public education, based on its state bureaucracies, has never been friendly to variety or diversity, so it is little wonder that the universities evolved in a similar fashion. That uniformity had been the product of the first education revolution of the 1860s and 1870s when the various colonies had inaugurated their different, but similar, systems of secular public education. Now the second education revolution launched by Menzies would seek individuality and variety but end up by yet again confirming the Australian talent for creating uniformity.

This is also the case with Menzies' other significant contribution to the second education revolution in Australia: the beginning of the funding of non-government schools. It is clear that Menzies had a soft spot for what he termed 'church schools', and his educational philosophy approved of the religious education that they provided for their students. Hence he made the following remarks at Mount Scopus College in Melbourne, in 1960:

I want to tell you, not for the first time, that I am a tremendous believer, an enthusiastic believer, in schools which have the background of religion; I think it is a marvellous thing that the boys and girls who are at this school and who will be at it in future, should be able to grow up adhering to their faith, knowing the foundations of their faith and keeping in contact with the great literary and religious tradition which serves to decorate that faith.[77]

Religious education, of whatever kind, helped to create good Australian citizens. However, the first Australian education revolution had created a 'secular' state system of education, which failed because it left Catholics outside the tent.[78] This exclusion, and the fact that Catholics had to pay both fees for their own schools and taxes to support state schools, was a significant ongoing sore in Australian public life. The Labor Party may have had many Catholic members of Parliament and supporters, but it failed to do anything to remedy what many saw as an injustice. On the other hand, one could argue that not receiving government largesse provided non-government schools with a certain independence.

These measures fitted easily into the Menzies vision of an educated Commonwealth. Funding science was a way of securing progress and national development in the material sense while scholarships for senior students was a way of ensuring that there would be an educated elite, based on merit, who would come to run the country. Again, it meshed well with Menzies' vision of the role education had to play in ensuring that Australian democracy had the leadership it required.

Looking back from the vantage point of the twenty-first century, it is easy to point to where Commonwealth funding of schools has led and, anachronistically, ask why Menzies ever bothered.

But that would be unfair. Menzies had a noble vision of education. It was a liberal vision and not narrowly Australian: 'The challenge to us as a nation to play our part in increasing the world's resources. And, in essence, that is a challenge to us to improve our education; for it is only by constantly improving education and skills that we discharge our world duty.'[79]

He was, as this chapter argues, in many ways an old-fashioned liberal with a philosophy grounded in idealism. It is true to say that Menzies had a vision of a harmonious organic society for Australia. A harmonious society was one composed of independent individuals who could come together and cooperate, recognising the benefits of being good citizens. They would elect leaders who equally worked for the public good; a good democracy required an educated and ethical elite to lead it.

He understood the role that education and, in particular, the universities had to play in ensuring that this type of modern democratic society worked as it should, for the benefit of the country and ultimately for the benefit of the world. Education was crucial to ensuring the project of Australian national development and progress. To this end Menzies helped to inaugurate what was essentially the second education revolution in Australia by providing funding for both public universities and independent schools. Both measures were guided by the desire to create a more harmonious Australia; the former by creating a leadership class that was both technically capable and ethically driven, the latter by seeking to put an end to a period of sectarian conflict that was one of the more unpleasant aspects of Australian life until the 1960s.

Menzies cannot be blamed for where the education revolution he helped to inaugurate ultimately led, except insofar as he failed to consider the financial implications of government funding of the universities. But then the British fell into exactly the same trap.

What one can say is that his educational policies were motivated by a generous vision about the future of Australia. One could wish that his generosity had been matched by those who were the beneficiaries of the changes that he brought into being.

CONCLUSION:
AUSTRALIAN LIBERALISM AND THE
FORGOTTEN MENZIES

For most of his career Menzies was not primarily interested in advocating the cause of liberalism and the principle of liberty; he was concerned to govern in an effective fashion for the benefit of all Australians so that they could peacefully and freely pursue their goals. He sought the reality of freedom, not the pursuit of a theoretical liberty. He could do so because he comprehended freedom, following Cardinal Newman, in a 'real' rather than a 'nominal' way.[1]

Menzies believed in the ideal of English freedom, which he saw as the basis of a dignified and civilised life. His understanding of freedom was embedded in his appreciation of a living culture in Australia, which, while it might not have been English, could be encompassed in the more general term 'British'. He was not ideological in a twenty-first-century sense but supported freedom as it was expressed in the day-to-day life of ordinary people. This can be seen clearly in the various addresses of his World War II speeches, most memorably in the 'Forgotten People'. Freedom—British freedom—was a lived experience that needed to be protected in a world threatened by forces which sought to destroy that freedom.

What freedom meant was not understood in a theoretical or ideological manner. It was not the liberty of an academic treatise. It was the possession of a people who instinctively knew how to behave in a manner befitting those who had been granted the precious gift of freedom. It expressed itself through such institutions as Parliament and the workings of the law. Unlike Americans, Australians had had no reason to question their British heritage or to universalise their political and legal concepts. They trusted in themselves rather than mechanisms and documents to protect their freedom. Menzies understood this principle perfectly: 'In short, responsible government in a democracy is regarded by us as the ultimate guarantee of justice and individual rights. Except for our inheritance of British institutions and the principles of the Common Law, we have not felt the need of formality and definition.'[2]

One could argue that, for Menzies, responsible government worked because it was composed of British puritans (including many of Irish extraction) who ensured that, through their behaviour, there was no 'need of formality and definition'.[3] Furthermore, there was an overriding commitment to duties more than rights. These puritans were also to be found on the labour side of politics, even if they called themselves 'socialists'. In 1948 Beatrice Webb wrote: 'The grant from the community to the individual, beyond what it does for all, ought to be conditional upon better conduct.'[4] With regard to early British theories of the welfare state, Michael Freeden has written of 'that puritan sense of duty, common in socialist ideology'.[5] Arthur Calwell, for example, in his autobiography launched into a denunciation of the 'permissive society'.[6]

Nevertheless, as indicated by his idealisation of both the English and of their universities, it would be true to say that a certain utopianism did underpin Menzies' largely non-ideological approach to politics. It is the same idealism that had drawn the young Keith Hancock into studying the British Commonwealth, then writing a defence of it during World War II. For men such as Menzies, Hancock and Eggleston, the British way was an antidote to the excesses of the age, including Nazism and communism. The English, argued Hancock in the 1930s, had remained 'medieval' while large parts of Europe succumbed to what Hancock termed 'Machiavellianism'. Following an idealised vision of Englishness seemed to offer an alternative vision of the good life and of a social order that would encompass harmony and justice. Commonwealth was, for Hancock, the solution to the problem of creating a just society that he had first posed in his book, *Australia*, published in 1930. It turned out to be just another utopian failure, a noble one nevertheless, but one that was doomed once the foundations of the British Empire began to crumble.

There is a strong connection between the British Commonwealth, as the empire was understood in dominions such as Australia, and cultural puritanism, which was closely aligned to Britishness as a form of civic religion. The real issue was whether this loosely connected set of values and ideals could survive once the British Empire had dissolved. The answer turned out to be no. World War II created the circumstances for the end of the empire. In retrospect, the fate of the empire can be seen to have been sealed at Munich in 1938 when the British made a massive miscalculation in not opposing Germany because of fear of the Soviet Union. The war exhausted Britain. The Britain of the 1930s that Menzies had idealised was no more.

But this took some time to manifest itself. Certainly, when Menzies became Prime Minister in 1949, it appeared to be business as usual. The Labor government that Menzies defeated had equally been Anglocentric in its outlook. After the shock of the 1930s and 1940s, the first decade of Menzies as Prime Minister was calm and sedate with Menzies maintaining a 'steady as it goes' approach. The Royal Visit of 1954 was a massive success, and Australia continued to send primary produce to Britain. But that decade was the calm before the storm. For one thing, Britain revived its agriculture, thereby reversing her earlier policy of using the dominions as her food baskets.

The 1960s was the key decade. It was the decade that saw, as Christian Champion puts it, 'the strange demise of British Canada'.[7] The threads that bound the Commonwealth disentangled. It was also the decade when secularisation quickened in Western countries, thereby dissolving older religious sentiments and practices. One might well consider that the decline in material power was matched by a decline in what might loosely be termed spiritual power. A potent symbol of that decline is the final scene of the 1968 movie *If*, in which disaffected students with machine guns mow down teachers, students and parents as they leave the school chapel. This was truly puritanism renounced and denounced.

During the 1940s and 1950s American intellectuals were noticing a decline in the virtues that constituted cultural puritanism. The most widely read example was Riesman, Glazer and Denney's *Lonely Crowd*, which described the decline of the 'inner-directed person':

> The inner-directed person, if influenced by Protestantism, is of course also unable to waste time. The mobile youth from the lower classes shows his commitment to inner direction by cutting himself off from hard-drinking, horse-play-indulging pals: he continues the production of an inner-directed character through practising a kind of mental bookkeeping by which the demons of Waste and Sloth are ruthlessly driven out. Such a person has little leisure, unless he can justify it as self-improving ...[8]

Soon after Riesman, Glazer and Denney's analysis was published, Australia would go down the path of Americanisation via the powerful cultural influence of television. A few years later, another widely read commentary on changing American character noted the 'decline of the Protestant ethic', being made up of 'hard, self-denying work' and 'self-reliance'.[9] By the 1950s Americans were quite used to nostalgic laments for a dying 'self-reliance' and 'rugged individualism'.[10] Post-war prosperity and technology was changing the Anglo character away from the cultural puritanism pined for by Menzies and social commentators in Britain and America. In 1962 one commentator on Australia could describe 'that youthful group whose international symbol is the espresso bar, whose mythic ideal is Elvis Presley and whose cultural values, superficially at least, have been formed by impressions from outside their community'. This group also practised a 'non-conformist sexual morality'.[11] Prosperity was producing a rights-centred individualism that would become radicalised during the Vietnam War era into multiple quasi-Marxist liberation movements. Liberation from what? The past: culture as it had been forged by its racial and gender elites. Much as cultural puritanism lasted for multiple generations, arguably, this liberation movement continues.[12]

Thus, one gets the sense that there was a certain disillusion in Menzies' later years after his retirement as he ceased to play much of a public role, unlike his successors as Prime Minister such as John Howard. This may have had much to do with developments in the British Commonwealth. In his two volumes of memoirs, Menzies preferred not to say much about Australian politics, especially about politicians or former politicians who were still alive. His most probing chapters discuss developments in the Commonwealth in the early 1960s and his disquiet that it had ceased to be a 'gentleman's club' and become ideological and political. His vision of the world, in which Englishness lay at the centre as the basis of a Commonwealth based on friendship, was coming apart with the collapse of the British Empire. In this context it is worth appreciating that Menzies' liberalism contained a powerful desire to create means that could temper the harshness of the world in the twentieth century.

It is also worth noting that Menzies had no fear of government *per se*; he believed in the capacity of government to work on behalf of Australia and do good for it. His period in office coincided with the golden age of the mandarin in Canberra with such figures as Roland Wilson, Frederick Wheeler and Arthur Tange. For Menzies, liberalism meant good government, and good government meant trusting senior public servants to work for the public good. It meant the creation of a meritocracy that ideally will have received a first-rate liberal education. A representative democracy meant elected representatives and mandarins working together to achieve the best for the country. The world might be harsh, but good men of an enlightened disposition could work together to overcome some of that harshness. Menzies would have hated the way in which politics since his time has become much more grounded in conflict and the constant striving for personal advantage.

Menzies' puritanism was an expression of a British Empire and of the Britishness that spread throughout that empire, especially in the years leading up to World War I. By the early 1960s it had become apparent that that world was on its last legs. In Australia, the key text expressing that demise was Donald Horne's *Lucky Country*. Horne attacked and condemned both Menzies and Calwell as yesterday's men who could not comprehend the contemporary world. Influenced by the abstract intellectualism that John Anderson had encouraged, Horne simply could not comprehend the puritan spirit that motivated such men. He wanted a new Australia in which so-called intellectuals, of which he considered himself one, would rule the roost.

Horne's lack of comprehension can be considered an indication of the death of the puritan personality and of the intellectual and spiritual understanding of the world that it embodied. Horne's book can be read as a manifesto of a post-puritan society, which would be much more ideological and intellectual than the one that had preceded it. Horne combined the harsh realism of John Anderson with an ideal of Australian nationalism as a liberation from the old-fashioned constraints of empire. The new nationalism easily turned into an expression of vulgarity, as can be seen in *Don's Party* and *Barry Mackenzie*, although its supposed embodiment, Gough Whitlam, was a man of dignity in the Menzies mould. In fact, it can be argued that Whitlam, despite his flaws, was the last embodiment of the dignity that had once characterised Australian prime ministers of all political persuasions.

Menzies' retirement in 1966 coincided with the end of the old Australian currency of zacs, tres and dinars, a measure that he had supported. Metrication commenced five years later. It was, in a real and concrete sense, the end of empire. Menzies was not averse to reform; he was the driving force behind the unsuccessful attempt to rid the Constitution of the nexus in 1967.[13] But, in many ways, for Menzies, as for Australia more generally, the end of empire was much closer to a revolution, although the real importance of this event is rarely recognised. The empire and the Commonwealth had been built on values of frugality, hard work, family and a strong sense of moral obligation. These were the values of cultural puritanism. Just as Hancock could describe the settled policies of Australian politics so it can be argued that Menzies embodied the cultural and social equivalent of those policies.

The 1960s and 1970s saw the unravelling of the settled cultural and policy practices, just as the 1980s saw the demise of the economic practices, both in Australia and elsewhere. To give some examples:

- Secularisation. The 1960s saw the beginning of the effective secularisation of Australian popular culture. This was just not in terms of a decline in church-going but also in such things as the liberalisation of laws regarding Sunday that had been in operation for hundreds of years. These came to encompass such things as entertainments on a Sunday and shop trading hours. The 'rest day' in Test cricket came to be no more. The old pattern of Sunday as a day of rest in which families came together for the Sunday roast declined.[14] The moral shifts that would also constitute secularisation were embodied in the 1977 Royal Commission on Human Relationships Final Report, commissioned by the Whitlam government. The report sought to place social policy on a basis of 'toleration', 'knowledge' and 'understanding', rather than 'dogma'. The more than 500 policy and legislative recommendations were essentially the abrogation of cultural puritanism in policy and legislation.[15]
- Affluenza. Patterns of frugality that had long marked Australian culture were eroded by a growing affluence and the increased availability of credit. By the 1970s the general public had gained access to credit cards. By the twenty-first century, banks that had once carefully screened potential borrowers were offering loans freely.
- Professionalisation and the decline of manufacturing. Australians were increasingly attaining higher levels of education. In part this was a consequence of Menzies' decision to provide Commonwealth funding for universities. A corollary of this change was the decline of workers in manual occupations, once a very significant part of the Australian workforce.[16]
- Multiculturalism. Although British Australia was still robust in the 1970s and 1980s, even in the metropolitan cities, official definitions of the Australian nation dropped Britishness for the more amorphous 'multiculturalism'.[17]

For the generation who grew to maturity in the 1960s, the old idea of H.B. Higgins of 'frugal comfort' expressed in his *Harvester* decision seemed outdated and a sign of how backward Australia had once been. The age of fibro was giving way to the age of brick veneer on the road to the McMansion.

Our interpretation of Menzies as the last cultural puritan is not intended to wholly supplant previous analyses, but rather to add to a growing body of literature that is uncovering his complexity, as well as the nuances of Australian social and political thinking before the culture wars. Menzies' puritan idealism further uncovers the specific nature of his Britishness, making greater sense of why he felt so comfortable identifying himself as a liberal yet rarely offered any positive appraisal of rights. The puritan and idealist tropes circulating in Australia during Menzies' formative years as well as the micro-culture of Menzies' Presbyterian–Methodist upbringing endowed him with a way of conceptualising civic virtue that lent itself to both conservative and liberal instincts.

Cultural puritanism was dying slowly during Menzies' own lifetime with the decline in Protestantism as a central part of British identity. S.J.D. Green argues that 'the political importance of religion in Britain declined markedly between 1920 and 1960'.[18] He gives three primary reasons for this development as follows: (1) the resolution of the Irish question; (2) the decline of the Nonconformist conscience; and (3) the rise of the Labour Party.[19] Of these three elements, Green places by the far the greatest emphasis on the removal of the Irish question from English politics. There were no longer Irish Catholic members of Parliament at Westminster; the end of the Irish question meant that the great enemy of British Protestantism since the time of Elizabeth, Catholicism, was gone from the scene forever.

It is worth noting that in the Australian context these three elements worked quite differently. The Labor Party was already fully

formed by 1920 and had held office as early as 1910. The Irish/
Catholic issue was not resolved in 1922 and took a quite different
form in Australia as Catholics generally identified with the Labor
Party. In the mid-1950s the sectarian issue flared up with the split
in the Labor Party and enormous acrimony regarding the role of
the 'Movement' as an agent of the Catholic Church. Finally, it
is possible to trace a decline in the Nonconformist conscience in
Australia, although the continuing presence of the 'Other' in the
shape of Catholicism helped to maintain Protestant identity at a
time when it might have faded. Furthermore, the rise of the welfare state, the affluence and consumerism that followed World
War II and the general secularisation of language and culture from
the 1950s onwards, especially from the mid-1960s, also helped to
make the puritan ethos and language obsolete.

Buried with cultural puritanism was Menzies' own legacy.
Whitlam embodied the post–World War II shift towards conceptualising citizenship in terms of rights and benefits rather than duties,
fully embodying Hancock's state-as-public-utility—everything
Menzies found objectionable about Labor.[20] In hindsight we can
see Menzies' career as a hopeless attempt to defend a dying dream
against inexorable secular trends eroding it: economic, technological, demographic and international. Thus, despite the difference
of six years between Menzies' retirement and Gough Whitlam's
accession to the office of Prime Minister, Whitlam's language of
rights and equality retains relevant to this day, while Menzies'
stress on independence and duties is obsolete and archaic.[21]

Certainly by the 1960s Menzies had a reputation as being at
best quaint and at worst a walking cultural fossil, and 'puritanism'
connoted hysterical moralism rather than sturdy independence.[22]
Although his effusive affection for the British Empire was entirely
in keeping with the sentiments of a majority of Australians in the
1950s, his admission that the centrality of Britain to Australian

and world affairs was finally ended was only painfully extracted.[23] During the last ten years of his life he was pessimistic about the future of Australia and the world, his two exercises in autobiography being exercises in nostalgia for a lost world or acerbity towards new emerging social and international trends.[24]

It must be said that Menzies' critics were by and large correct in their assessment of his failed legacy, and the tone of his two exercises in autobiography would suggest that he knew they were correct. But contrary to many unsympathetic accounts of Menzies, most obviously that of Donald Horne, Menzies was not oblivious to the secular trends that were fading his idyllic vision of puritan Australia. Indeed, Menzies, like his contemporary idealist philosophers, spent a good deal of time warning Australians of the potentially corrosive cultural effects of affluence and faith in technology rather than human spirit as he conceived it. But to say that Menzies' vision for Australia failed is not merely to say that puritan Britishness declined as a formative influence over our culture and sense of national identity. It is also to say that individualistic rights, affluenza, political apathy and cultural philistinism—all the trends Menzies was at pains to ward off—triumphed. Seen in this light, even Menzies' critics might concede that the failure of his vision is not wholly to be celebrated. Perhaps even the members of the 'party of progress' will consider that 'progress' meant something different to Menzies than it does now. Perhaps in our tribalised and self-righteous age honest—even solemn—self-scrutiny among political and ideological partisans is the most fitting and truly progressive way to pay respect to Australia's longest-serving Prime Minister.

NOTES

INTRODUCTION

1 G. Melleuish & S.A. Chavura, 'Utilitarianism contra sectarianism: The official and the unauthorized civic religion of Australia', in *Only in Australia: The History, Politics and Economics of Australian Exceptionalism*, ed. W. Coleman, Oxford University Press, Oxford, 2016, p. 77.

2 P. Keating, 'Gough broke "Menzian torpor": Keating', *SBS News*, 21 October 2014.

3 See G. Melleuish, 'E.G. Whitlam: Reclaiming the initiative in Australian history', in *Making Modern Australia: The Whitlam Government's 21st Century Agenda*, ed. J. Hocking, Monash University Press, Clayton, 2017, pp. 308–35.

4 See S. Benson, 'Battle to claim the Menzies legacy a shot across the bow', *Australian*, 11 July 2017.

5 P. Van Onselen, 'Liberal Party reactionaries ignore Menzies' progressive vision', *Australian*, 17 February 2017.

6 R.G. Menzies, *Afternoon Light: Some Memories of Men and Events*, Cassell, Melbourne, 1967, p. 6.

7 D. Kemp, 'Liberalism, conservatism and the growth of government in Australia', in *Liberalism and Conservatism*, ed. G. Melleuish, Connor Court, Ballarat, 2015, p. 82.

8 D. Freeman, *Abbott's Right: The Conservative Tradition from Menzies to Abbott*, Melbourne University Press, Carlton, 2017.

9 S.A. Chavura & G. Melleuish, 'Conservative instinct in Australian political thought: The Federation debates, 1890–1898', *Australian Journal of Political Science*, vol. 50, no. 3, pp. 513–28.

10 W.K. Hancock, *Australia* [1930], Ernest Benn, London, 1945, pp. 42, 44, 177, 234.

11 B. Chifley, 'Petrol rationing—An unpopular duty', in *Things Worth Fighting For: Speeches by Joseph Benedict Chifley*, ed. A.W. Stargardt, Melbourne University Press, Melbourne, 1952, p. 177.

12 On Menzies as a civic republican, see A. Carr & B.T. Jones, 'Civic republicanism and Sir Robert Menzies: The non-liberal side of the Liberal leader', *Journal of Australian Studies*, vol. 37, no. 4, 2013, pp. 485–502.

13 A.A. Calwell, *Be Just and Fear Not*, Lloyd O'Neil, Melbourne, 1972, pp. 243–9.

14 Freeman, *Abbott's Right*.

15 Throughout this manuscript the terms 'idealist' and 'idealism' refer to a specific trend or school of philosophical thinking, as outlined in chapter 2.

16 See chapter 4.

17 J.H. Newman, *Apologia Pro Vita Sua: Being a History of His Religious Opinions*, Oxford University Press, London, 1964, p. 25.

18 All of which may be found at: http://docs.fdrlibrary.marist.edu/firesi90.html.

19 Available at: http://voicesofdemocracy.umd.edu/fdr-the-four-freedoms-speech-text/

20 B. Chifley, 'For freedom', in *Justice Now! Social Justice Statements of the Australian Catholic Bishops 1940–1966*,

ed. M. Hogan, Department of Government and Public Administration, University of Sydney, Sydney, 1990, pp. 26–37.

21 D. Horne, *The Lucky Country: Australia in the Sixties* [1964], Penguin, Harmondsworth, 2nd edn, 1968, p. 101.

22 In the second edition of *The Lucky Country*, Horne calls Calwell a fundamentalist, as opposed to being an adherent of the 'new leftism' that had emerged by the late 1960s, particularly in response to the Vietnam War (p. 183). Horne accurately saw that the radicalism of the 1960s—tamed and institutionalised in the Whitlam government (1972–75)—saw Menzies' Liberal Party and Calwell's Labor Party as equally reactionary.

23 J. Belich, *Replenishing the Earth: The Settler Revolution and the Rise of the Anglo World, 1783–1939*, Oxford University Press, Oxford, 2009.

24 D. Malouf, 'Australia's British inheritance', in *Four Classic Quarterly Essays on the Australian Story*, Black Inc., Melbourne, 2006, p. 19.

25 M.G.S. Hodgson, *Rethinking World History: Essays on Europe, Islam and World History*, Cambridge University Press, Cambridge, 1993, ch. 8.

26 Chavura & Melleuish, 'Conservative instinct in Australian political thought'.

27 1891 Sydney Federation Convention. Cited in ibid., p. 8.

28 R.G. Menzies, *Central Power in the Australian Commonwealth*, Cassell, London, 1967, p. 50.

29 J.A. La Nauze & Elizabeth Nurser (eds), *Walter Murdoch and Alfred Deakin on Books and Men: Letters and Comments 1900–1918*, Melbourne University Press, Melbourne, 1974.

30 J. Murphy, *Evatt: A Life*, NewSouth, Sydney, 2016, p. 35.

31 R.G. Menzies, *The Measure of the Years*, Cassell, London, 1970, ch. 21.

32 On Chisholm, see S. Scott, 'Chisholm, Alan Rowland (1888–1981)', *Australian Dictionary of Biography*, National Centre of Biography, Australian National University.

33 M. Hughes-Warrington and I. Tregenza, 'State and civilization in Australian new idealism, 1890–1950', *History of Political Thought*, vol. 29, no. 1, 2008, pp. 89–108.

34 See R.G. Menzies, *The Changing Commonwealth*, Cambridge University Press, Cambridge, 1960.

35 W.M. Hughes, *Crusts and Crusades*, Angus & Robertson, Sydney, 1948.

36 J.C. Smuts, *Holism and Evolution*, Macmillan, London, 1927, p. 273.

37 F.W. Eggleston, *Search for a Social Philosophy*, Melbourne University Press, Melbourne, 1941, p. 54.

38 La Nauze & Nurser, *Walter Murdoch and Alfred Deakin*, p. 36.

39 In fact there was a strong idealist tradition of speaking of personality as spirit. Hegel's own Geist must have been influential, but we also read the following from the American idealist philosopher and correspondent of Sir Alfred Deakin, Josiah Royce: 'The resulting doctrine of life and of the nature of truth and of reality which I have tried to work out, to connect with logical and metaphysical issues and to teach to my classes, now seems to me not so much romanticism, as a fondness for defining, for articulating and for expounding the perfectly real, concrete and literal life of what we idealists call the "spirit", in a sense which is indeed Pauline ...' ('Words of Professor Royce at the Walton Hotel at Philadelphia, December 29, 1915', *The Philosophy of Josiah Royce*, ed. J.K. Roth, Thomas Y. Crowell Co., New York, 1971, pp. 406–7).

1 CULTURAL PURITANISM IN YOUNG MENZIES' AUSTRALIA

1 Colley makes the connection between cultural puritanism and Margaret Thatcher via Thatcher's father: 'a Methodist

grocer', 'a self-made man', with 'conspicuously puritan morality, Spartan lifestyle and commitment to duty' (L. Colley, *Britons: Forging the Nation: 1707–1837* [1992], 2nd edn, Yale University Press, New Haven and London, 2005, p. 368).

2 See S.A. Chavura, J. Gascoigne & I. Tregenza, *Reason, Religion and the Australian Polity: A Secular State?* Routledge, London, 2019, ch. 5.

3 See D. Kemp, *The Land of Dreams: How Australians Won their Freedom 1788–1860*, Miegunyah Press, Carlton, 2018, pp. 65–6. On evangelicalism and the construction of civil society in colonial Australia, see S. Piggin & R.D. Linder, *The Fountain of Public Prosperity: Evangelical Christians in Australian History 1740–1914*, Monash University Publishing, Clayton, 2018.

4 J. West, *Union among the Colonies*, ed. G. Melleuish, Australian Scholarly Publishing, Kew, Vic, 2001; R.G. Ely, 'The religion of John West: Orthodox Protestant, deist, atheist, or what?', *Lucas: An Evangelical History Review*, nos 25 & 26, 1999, pp. 46–74.

5 For the relationship between Lang's political ideas and his Calvinism, see Chavura, Gascoigne & Tregenza, *Reason, Religion and the Australian Polity*, pp. 84–9.

6 Like many good Enlightened Englishmen, Parkes saw the struggle for general education partly in terms of a 'battle' between 'that of Protestantism and Progress against Roman Catholic Usurpation and Regression' (Henry Parkes to J.D. Lang, 27 November 1868, cited in A.W. Martin, 'Faction, politics and the education question in New South Wales', in *Melbourne Studies in Education, 1960–61*, ed. E.L. French, Melbourne University Press, Melbourne, 1962, p. 37. See also A.W. Martin, *Henry Parkes: A Biography*, Melbourne University Press, Carlton, 1980, pp. 105–6).

7   Menzies was often called upon to perform his imitation of the evangelical wowser preacher William Henry Judkins. See Piggin & Linder, *The Fountain of Public Prosperity*, p. 470.

8   H.G.R. Robinson, *Speeches Delivered by His Excellency Sir Hercules G.R. Robinson*, Gibbs, Shallard & Company, Sydney, 1879, p. 131.

9   M.P. Winship, *Godly Republicanism: Puritans, Pilgrims and a City on a Hill*, Harvard University Press, Cambridge, MA, 2012.

10 J. Hirst, *The Strange Birth of Colonial Democracy: New South Wales 1848–1884*, Allen & Unwin, North Sydney, 1988.

11 J. Brett, *Australian Liberals and the Moral Middle Class: From Alfred Deakin to John Howard*, Cambridge University Press, Cambridge, 2003, p. 41.

12 D.W.A. Baker, *Days of Wrath: A Life of John Dunmore Lang*, Melbourne University Press, Carlton, 1985, ch. 16.

13 'It is as much a matter for the sacred circle of home as any other duty devolving upon the member of a free community. Are not the women and children interested in the election of men to make laws for them? The subject is one which the good citizen will not scorn to talk over with his wife—which no sensible woman will wish her husband to regard with indifference' (H. Parkes, *The Electoral Act and How to Work It: A Series of Letters on the Subject of the Approaching Elections*, Sydney, 1859, p. 17). A.W. Martin speaks of the 'puritanism which interlaced radical thinking in the colony' in connection with Parkes' moral attack on Governor Sir Charles FitzRoy's circle of associates (Martin, *Henry Parkes*, p. 122).

14 Piggin & Linder, *The Fountain of Public Prosperity*.

15 Patrick McMahon Glynn, Catholic and South Australian delegate to the Federation conventions in the 1890s, could complain to his diary on a Sunday night that 'The dull peace of

the Puritan Sabbath oppresses the place' (diary entry, 29 October 1898, Patrick McMahon Glynn Papers, National Library of Australia [hereafter NLA], MS 4653, Box 1, Series 3).

16 R. Samuel, 'The discovery of Puritanism, 1820–1914: A preliminary sketch', in *Revival and Religion since 1700: Essays for John Walsh*, ed. J. Garnett and C. Matthew, Bloomsbury Academic, London, 1993, pp. 201–47. Cited in M. Grimley, 'The religion of Englishness: Puritanism, providentialism and "national character", 1918–1945', *Journal of British Studies*, vol. 46, no. 4, 2007, p. 896, f.n. 74.

17 Grimley, 'The religion of Englishness', p. 896.

18 E. Shann, *Bond or Free? Occasional Economic Essays*, Angus & Robertson, Sydney, 1930. Hancock was an assistant lecturer in Shann's department at the University of Western Australia in 1921. Hancock also helped Shann in some of the research for his economic history of Australia. See J. Davidson, *A Three-cornered Life: The Historian W.K. Hancock*, UNSW Press, Sydney, 2010, pp. 37–8.

19 S.J.D. Green, *The Passing of Protestant England: Secularisation and Social Change c. 1920–1960*, Cambridge University Press, Cambridge, 2011.

20 Although by no means a second-wave feminist, Menzies was, for a man born in 1894, ahead of his times in terms of including women as legitimate participants in cultural and political institutions. As early as 1916 we find the undergraduate Menzies consciously speaking of 'we University men and women' and of his own Melbourne University as 'an institution, giving instruction to those whom we may surely and in all humility, describe as some of the ablest men and women of the blossoming generation'. No one would have batted an eyelid had Menzies stuck to the universally accepted (and expected) masculine personal pronoun. References are respectively from:

R.G. Menzies, 'Education and truth', *Melbourne University Magazine (MUM)*, vol. X, no. 1, 1916, p. 5; R.G. Menzies, 'The place of the university in the life of the state', *Melbourne University Review*, vol. X, no. 2, 1916, pp. 37–8. See also Menzies' essay 'Women in war', published in his *Forgotten People and Other Studies in Democracy*, Angus & Robertson, Sydney, 1943, pp. 85–9.

21 Parkes said in around 1859 or 1860 that, as a newspaper editor, 'I attempted ... to implant an austere spirit of independence into the public press and to infuse into our infant liberties a true British vigour and purity' (cited in Martin, *Henry Parkes*, p. 173).

22 H. Parkes, *Mr Gladstone and English Liberalism from an Australian Point of View*, Lee & Ross, Sydney, 1878, p. 12.

23 For Macrossan, see *Official Record of the Proceedings and Debates of the Australasian Federation Conference, 1890*, Robert S. Brain, Government Printer, Victoria, 1890, p. 199. For Parkes, see ibid., pp. 217–18.

24 S. Macintyre, *A Colonial Liberalism: The Lost World of Three Victorian Visionaries*, Oxford University Press, Melbourne, 1991, p. 5.

25 'Untitled notes on a lecture on religion', n.d., p. C. Charles Henry Pearson Papers, State Library of Victoria, Box 436/1, MS57153.

26 T.G. Tucker, *Platform Monologues*, Thomas C. Lothian, Melbourne, 1914, pp. 191–2.

27 J. Rickard, *H.B. Higgins: The Rebel as Judge*, Allen & Unwin, Sydney, 1984, p. 201.

28 'Sympathy' ornaments all of Woolley's published speeches, as it did much British Enlightenment moralising in general. For example, see *Inaugural Address [delivered in] Maitland, on the opening of [the School of Arts]*, Robert Wisdom and

the *Northern Times*, Maitland, NSW, 1857, p. 6. See also G. Melleuish, 'The theology and philosophy of John Woolley', *Journal of Religious History*, vol. 12, no. 4, 1983, pp. 418–32.

29 This is the crux of the complex and rich argument of Eggleston's *Search for a Social Philosophy*.

30 Hughes-Warrington & Tregenza, 'State and civilization in Australian new idealism, 1890–1950'.

31 A. Deakin, *The Federal Story: The Inner History of the Federal Cause*, Robertson & Mullens, Melbourne, 1944, p. 65.

32 Ibid., p. 66.

33 Ibid., p. 130. 'Comtist': an adherent of the philosophy of Auguste Comte (1798–1857).

34 W. Murdoch, *Alfred Deakin* [1923], Bookman Press, Melbourne, 1999, p. 292.

35 Brett, *Australian Liberals and the Moral Middle Class*.

36 See D.R. Gibbs, 'Victorian school books: A study of the changing social content and use of school books in Victoria, 1848–1948, with particular reference to school readers', PhD thesis, University of Melbourne, 1987, pp. 197–200.

37 School Paper (Class IV), vol. 2, no. 20, March 1899, pp. 143–4. Cited in ibid., p. 198.

38 *Argus*, 23 September 1905, p. 12.

39 *Argus*, 23 April 1909, p. 6.

40 *Age*, 24 January 1914, p. 4.

41 *Age*, 1 December 1917, p. 6.

42 *Argus*, 10 December 1923, p. 9.

43 'The English race', *Age*, 18 April 1931, p. 10.

44 Hancock published an article, 'Classics', in the *Melbourne University Magazine*, vol. XI, no. 2, 1917, pp. 49–51.

45 Hancock, *Australia*, p. 42.

46 Ibid., p. 44.

47 'Empire creators: Our debt to the British merchants', *Age*, 8 January 1927, p. 21.

48 He publicly referred to his own 'deep-seated Presbyterianism'. At times he could playfully allude to the famous First Question of the Westminster Catechism—the Presbyterians' Credo—to make a point: '... the chief end of the State becomes man'; 'We are not to adapt the Shorter catechism to read "The chief end of men is to glorify science and enjoy it forever."' '... the chief end of totalitarianism is to glorify power and enjoy it forever.' First quote from 'Address by the Prime Minister, Rt Hon. Robert Menzies at the Pleasant Sunday Afternoon, Central Methodist Mission, Melbourne, Sunday, 7 September 1958, p. 1. Robert Menzies Papers, NLA, MS 4936, Box 265, Folder 103; second quote from 'The nature of democracy', *The Forgotten People*, p. 172; third quote from 'Modern science and civilization' (1958), in *Speech is of Time: Selected Speeches and Writings*, Cassell, London, 1958, p. 245; fourth quote from 'Freedom in modern society' [n.d.; 1935–36?]', p. 5, Robert Menzies Papers, NLA, MS 4936, Box 251, Folder 4. This speech is also printed in *Speech is of Time*, although the date is listed as unknown, but see the justification for the date listed in the manuscript version on p. 11.

49 'The power of Presbyterianism', *Argus*, 16 September 1933, p. 22.

2 THE IDEALIST MILIEU

1 On Green's puritanism, see A. De Sanctis, *The 'Puritan' Democracy of Thomas Hill Green*, Imprint Academic, Exeter, 2005.

2 Cited in A.N. Wilson, *God's Funeral*, Abacus, London, 1999, p. 274.

3 M. Sawer, *The Ethical State? Social Liberalism in Australia*, Melbourne University Press, Carlton, 2003, p. 14.

4 Examination to be found in John Latham Papers, NLA, MS 1009, Box 45. John Latham, later judge on the High Court,

was a student of Laurie, calling him the 'best of the Profs'. See A.G. Smith, 'Laurie, Henry (1837–1922)', *Australian Dictionary of Biography*, National Centre of Biography, Australian National University.

5 Hughes-Warrington & Tregenza, 'State and civilization in Australian new idealism, 1890–1950'. On the influence of British idealism on Australian thought, see J. Franklin, *Corrupting the Youth: A History of Philosophy in Australia*, Macleay Press, Sydney, 2003, chs 6–7; Sawer, *The Ethical State?*. Wayne Hudson discusses the distinctives of Australian idealism in *Australian Religious Thought*, Monash University Press, Clayton, 2016, pp. 132–46, esp. p. 136.

6 Such as Catholic natural law theory, utopian socialism and quasi-religious theories of labour relations. See Chavura, Gascoigne & Tregenza, *Reason, Religion and the Australian Polity*, ch. 7. See Hudson's *Australian Religious Thought* in general.

7 As famously stated by H. Collins, 'Political ideology in Australia: The distinctiveness of a Benthamite society', in *The Daedalus Symposium*, ed. S.R. Graubard, Angus & Robertson, Sydney, 1985, pp. 147–69. That Australian institutional and national culture is best described as utilitarian is one of the settled doctrines of Australian historiography. The problem is not so much that it is wrong but that the term 'utilitarian' is so open to serious misunderstanding that analyses of Australian culture as utilitarian frequently mischaracterise the culture and institutions as secularist and Benthamite. This is understandable in some ways, as most scholars encounter the utilitarian tradition in philosophy or economics units, both of which focus, understandably, on the utilitarianism of Jeremy Bentham and J.S. Mill, two of the tradition's greatest and most sophisticated exponents. The problem is

that utilitarianism as a movement was much broader than Bentham and Mill, both of whom were uncharacteristically secular for their ages. Hence it is a cardinal error from the point of view of intellectual history to assume that utilitarians of the eighteenth and nineteenth centuries, or those who believed they were simply promoting the greatest happiness for the greatest number, were therefore secularists, Benthamites or Millites. In fact, a tradition of Christian utilitarianism stretched at least as far back as the writings of the much-read Church of England intellectual William Paley (1743–1805), whose thought was much more in keeping with mainstream culture than either Bentham or Mill, even if the latter two utilitarians offered versions of the philosophy that turned out to be more appealing to modern philosophers and economists. Once we understand the richness of the utilitarian movement of the eighteenth and nineteenth centuries, looking beyond the standard texts of Bentham and Mill, we see how problematic it is to assume that Australian intellectual, institutional and national cultures were secularist or Benthamite because they were utilitarian. As always, history—even intellectual history—done from the philosopher's armchair will do little to illuminate the complexity and richness of the real world. We have questioned the utilitarian thesis elsewhere. See Chavura & Melleuish, 'Conservative instinct in Australian political thought'; Melleuish & Chavura, 'Utilitarianism contra sectarianism'; see also Chavura, Gascoigne & Tregenza, *Reason, Religion and the Australian Polity*, pp. 9, 27–32, 92–3. See also C. Berg, 'Adam Smith and Jeremy Bentham in the Australian colonies', *History of Economics Review*, vol. 68, no. 1, 2017, pp. 2–16.

8 On theosophy and spiritualism in general, see the standard work by J. Roe, *Beyond Belief: Theosophy in Australia*

1879–1939, UNSW Press, Sydney, 1986. More recently see Hudson, *Australian Religious Thought*, references to theosophy and spiritualism throughout.

9 M. Hearn, 'A transnational imagination: Alfred Deakin's reading lists', in *Transnational Ties: Australian Lives in the World*, ed. D. Deacon, P. Russell & A. Woollacott, ANU E-Press, Canberra, 2008, para. with f.n. 33.

10 H. Jones, *Idealism as a Practical Creed*, James Maclehose & Sons, Glasgow, 1909, p. 138.

11 Hearn, 'A transnational imagination'.

12 Most recently see J. Brett, *The Enigmatic Mr Deakin*, Text Publishing, Melbourne, 2017, ch. 4: 'The plunge into spiritualism'.

13 'I take it that the "atom bomb" is an example of the weapons which are furnished by inquiry to destructiveness—weapons the use of which may destroy civilization and thus inquiry itself. It seems to me quite possible that we have entered a period of cultural degeneration, that we are approaching one of Vico's "new barbarisms".' J. Anderson, 'The one good' [1945], *Studies in Empirical Philosophy*, Angus & Robertson, Sydney, 1962, p. 290.

14 On the Andersonian impact, see Franklin, *Corrupting the Youth*, ch. 1.

15 Hughes-Warrington & Tregenza, 'State and civilization in Australian new idealism, 1890–1950', p. 92.

16 'He had a malicious but devastating wit. In my time, his contributions to discussion in Cabinet were almost invariably destructive' (Menzies, *Afternoon Light*, p. 109).

17 R.G. Menzies, 'What are we fighting for?', *Melbourne University Magazine*, vol. 10, no. 3, 1916, p. 74. Original italics.

18 Hughes-Warrington & Tregenza, 'State and civilization in Australian new idealism, 1890–1950', p. 94.

19 T.H. Green, *Lectures on the Principles of Political Obligation and Other Writings*, ed. P. Harris & J. Morrow, Cambridge University Press, Cambridge, 1986. See also I. Tregenza, 'From virtues to values: Conceptions of Australian citizenship', in *From Migrant to Citizen: Testing Language, Testing Culture*, ed. C. Slade & M. Möllering, Palgrave Macmillan, London, 2010, p. 61.

20 'Smawnsh', 'Have we any culture?', *Melbourne University Magazine*, vol. X, no. 1, 1916.

21 Aladdin, 'Science and mind', *Melbourne University Magazine*, vol. 10, no. 3, 1916, p. 90.

22 Menzies, 'Education and truth', p. 4.

23 'But the older and more definite religious beliefs that meant so much to these men were being successfully attacked by the "Agnostics" of the same period. Yet even the "Agnostics" were puritan in feeling and in outlook. Matthew Arnold, the prophet of "culture", spoke of "conduct" as "three parts of life"' (G.M. Trevelyan, *English Social History: A Survey of Six Centuries, Chaucer to Queen Victoria*, Longmans, Green & Co., London, 1942, p. 563).

24 Menzies, 'The place of the university in the life of the state', p. 38.

25 Although Murdoch would become Professor of Literature at the University of Western Australia in 1913, until then his formative years intellectually were spent immersed in the Melbourne intellectual scene and as an assistant lecturer at Melbourne University. Menzies quoted Murdoch on at least one occasion. See Menzies' undated speech, 'The general moral rule', p. 1, Robert Menzies Papers, NLA, MS 4936, Box 251, Folder 2.

26 W. Murdoch, *The Australian Citizen: An Elementary Account of Civic Rights and Duties*, Whitcombe & Tombs, Melbourne, 1912, p. 75.

27 Ibid., p. 233.

28 Eggleston, *Search for a Social Philosophy*, p. 302.

29 Ibid., p. 325.

30 Ibid., p. 321.

31 Hancock, *Australia*, p. 136.

32 Ibid., p. 61.

33 Ibid., pp. 61–2.

34 Ibid., p. 234.

35 Undated manuscript in Robert Menzies Papers, NLA, MS 4936, Box 251, Folder 2. The thoughts expressed by Smuts in this manuscript epitomise much of Menzies' thought and language, not just in his 'Forgotten People' speeches but also in his public thought in general: 'There is today a decay of the individual's responsibility and share in government which seems to strike at the roots of our human advance.' Or: 'For me the individual is basic to any world-order that is worth while. Individual freedom, individual independence of mind, individual participation in the different work of government seems to me essential to all true progress.'

36 'Freedom in modern society' [n.d.; 1935–36?], p. 13, Robert Menzies Papers, NLA, MS 4936, Box 251, Folder 4.

3 THE *FORGOTTEN PEOPLE* SPEECHES

1 Trevelyan, *English Social History*, p. 493.

2 Ibid., p. 563.

3 'Freedom in modern society' [n.d.; 1935–36?], p. 16, Robert Menzies Papers, NLA, MS 4936, Box 251, Folder 4. See this speech also printed in *Speech is of Time*.

4 'The ethics of popular self-government', pp. 7–8, Robert Menzies Papers, NLA, MS 4936, Box 251, Folder 2. This typescript has Menzies' cursive in the top left corner, reading: 'Church talks to individuals. Its work is with the individual

character, not with individual things as such. Render unto Caesar. Luke 20–22.'

5   Ibid., p. 8.

6   T.G. Tucker, Professor of Classical Philology at the University of Melbourne, has an essay entitled 'Hebraism and Hellenism' in his collection *Platform Monologues* (1914). The idea of a 'Hebrew element' goes back to Matthew Arnold.

7   'The English character, Hatchard's Bookshop, Tuesday March 25th 1941', in *'To the People of Britain at War': From the Prime Minister of Australia. Speeches by the Right Honourable Robert Gordon Menzies delivered in Great Britain in 1941*, Longmans, Green & Co., London, 1941, p. 56.

8   Copy of personal confidential diary for Overseas Journey— 19/2/35–8/9/35, p. 71, Robert Menzies Papers, NLA, MS 4936, Box 572 [no folder].

9   On whether there was 'room at [royal] Court for philosophy', Sir Thomas More wrote, 'There's certainly no room for the academic variety, which says what it thinks irrespective of circumstances. But there is a more civilized form of philosophy which knows the dramatic context, so to speak, tries to fit in with it and plays the appropriate part in the current performance' (*Utopia* [1516], trans. P. Turner, Penguin, Harmondsworth, 1965, p. 63).

10 G. Santayana, 'Soliloquies in England' [1922], *The Philosophy of Santayana*, ed. I. Edman, Modern Library, New York, 1936, p. 356.

11 R. Williams, *Culture and Society 1780–1950* [1958], Pelican, London, 1971.

12 J. Brett, *Robert Menzies' Forgotten People*, Melbourne University Press, Carlton, 2nd edn, 2007, p. 41.

13 His papers, however, indicate some acquaintance with popular writings on Marxism. See 'Communism and Christianity

[1946 broadcast]', Robert Menzies Papers, NLA, MS 4936, Box 256, Folder 35.

14 W.K. Hancock, *Argument of Empire*, Penguin, Harmondsworth, p. 107.

15 Brett, *Robert Menzies' Forgotten People*, p. 59; cf. p. 61. Menzies uses the word 'independence' or 'independent' at least nine times throughout *The Forgotten People*, and the concept pervades the entire book with other words such as 'self-reliance'.

16 Ibid., p. 59.

17 Ibid., p. 47.

18 Most fully explored in M. Todd, *Christian Humanism and Puritan Social Order*, Cambridge University Press, Cambridge, 1987.

19 'The forgotten people', *The Forgotten People and Other Studies in Democracy* [hereafter *FP*], p. 8.

20 Ibid., p. 2.

21 'The government and ourselves', *FP*, p. 145.

22 'Taxing the shareholder', *FP*, p. 107.

23 Ibid., p. 111; cf. 'Is inflation a bogey?', *FP*, p. 122.

24 'The task of democracy', *FP*, p. 186.

25 'The forgotten people', *FP*, p. 5.

26 'The government and ourselves', *FP*, p. 145.

27 'The forgotten people', *FP*, p. 4.

28 Ibid.

29 Ibid., p. 5.

30 'Empire control of an empire war', *FP*, p. 41.

31 'The task of democracy', *FP*, p. 184; 'The importance of cheerfulness', *FP*, p. 189.

32 'The task of democracy', *FP*, pp. 187–8.

33 'The forgotten people', *FP*, p. 5.

34 'Freedom of speech and expression', *FP*, pp. 11–12. He repeated the point in his discussion of freedom of religion: 'Freedom of religion', *FP*, p. 22.

35 Ibid., p. 14.

36 'Freedom from want', *FP*, p. 28.

37 'Compulsory unionism', *FP*, p. 128.

38 'Forgotten people', *FP*, p. 14.

39 'The achievements of democracy', *FP*, p. 180.

40 Cf. ibid., p. 183.

41 'The Christian citizen in a new era', speech delivered at St Columba Presbyterian Church, Woollahra, NSW, 11am, Sunday 27 February 1944, p. 2, Robert Menzies Papers, NLA, MS 4936, Box 253, Folder 13.

42 Ibid., pp. 2–3.

43 'Forgotten People', *FP*, p. 2.

44 Eggleston, *Search for a Social Philosophy*, p. 324.

45 Ibid., p. 327.

46 'The forgotten people', *FP*, p. 2.

47 'Has capitalism failed?', *FP*, p. 5.

48 'Compulsory unionism', *FP*, p. 130.

49 Menzies used the term 'citizen' many times throughout *The Forgotten People* and 'citizenship' less so.

50 Menzies quoted Murdoch (who was paraphrasing Kant) in an undated speech entitled 'The general moral rule': 'Act in such a way as, upon mature consideration, you think it good for the State that all its citizens should act' (Robert Menzies Papers, NLA, MS 4936, Box 251, Folder 2).

51 R.G. Menzies, 'Is democracy doomed?', broadcast address for the ABC [n.d.; mid-1930s?], p. 4, Robert Menzies Papers, NLA, MS 4936, Box 151, Folder 5.

52 'The nature of democracy', *FP*, p. 172.

53 Ibid., p. 173.

54 'The achievements of democracy', *FP*, p. 183.

55 'The task of democracy', *FP*, p. 185.

56 Ibid., p. 186.

57 We discuss education and the universities more fully in chapter 5.

58 'The task of democracy', *FP*, p. 187.

59 'Paying for the war', *FP*, p. 91.

60 'Taxing the shareholder', *FP*, p. 107.

61 'Compulsory unionism', *FP*, p. 128.

62 Ibid., p. 129.

63 Ibid., p. 128.

64 'The government and ourselves', *FP*, p. 143.

65 Ibid., p. 143.

66 Ibid., p. 145.

67 'Compulsory unionism', *FP*, p. 130.

68 'The moral element in total war', *FP*, p. 161.

69 Eggleston, *Search for a Social Philosophy*, p. 329.

70 'The nature of democracy', *FP*, p. 170.

71 In which Churchill linked the Battle of Britain with the 'survival of Christian civilization' (cited in J. Wolffe, *God and Greater Britain: Religion and National Life in Britain and Northern Ireland 1843–1945*, Routledge, London, 1994, p. 250).

72 'Speech by the Hon. R.G. Menzies on education', from the Parliamentary Debates, 26 July 1945, Robert Menzies Papers, NLA, MS 4936, Box 253, Folder 15.

73 B. Penton, *Think or Be Damned: A Subversive Note on National Pride, Patriotism and Other Forms of Ostrichism Practised in Australia*, Angus & Robertson, Sydney, 1941. The book was republished every year from 1941 to 1945.

74 'The moral element in total war', *FP*, pp. 161–2.

75 Ibid.

76 Ibid.

77 Ibid., p. 164.

78 'Hatred as an instrument of war policy', *FP*, p. 53.

79 Ibid., p. 54.

80 Ibid., p. 55.

81 Ibid., p. 56.

82 Ibid.

83 Ibid., pp. 56–7.

84 'The drink problem', *FP*, p. 117.

85 Ibid., p. 119.

4 CHRISTIANITY, DEMOCRACY AND CIVILISATION

1 'Speech in the Great Hall, Houses of Parliament, London' (4 July 35), p. 1, Robert Menzies Papers, NLA, MS 4936, Box 251, Folder 4.

2 Copy of personal confidential diary for Overseas Journey—19/2/35–8/9/35, p. 37, Robert Menzies Papers, NLA, MS 4936, Box 572. Italics added.

3 'Civic service, speech at Presbyterian Church, Cheltenham, Victoria, 4 April 1965', p. 1, Robert Menzies Papers, NLA, MS 4936, Box 576, Folder: Speeches 1964–66.

4 Menzies, *Afternoon Light*, p. 286.

5 Ibid.

6 'The forgotten people', *FP*, p. 3.

7 'The four freedoms: Freedom from fear', *FP*, p. 34.

8 'The four freedoms: Freedom from fear (continued)', *FP*, p. 35.

9 'The forgotten people', *FP*, p. 5.

10 Ibid.

11 See G. Melleuish, *Despotic State or Free Individual: Two Traditions of Democracy in Australia*, Australian Scholarly Publishing, Melbourne, 2014, especially ch. 3.

12 Ibid., especially chs 5 & 7.

13 See *Official Report of the National Australasian Convention Debates (Third Session): Melbourne 1898*, Robert S. Brain, Government Printer, Melbourne, 1898, pp. 3533–8.

14 Melleuish, *Despotic State or Free Individual*, pp. 111–12.

15 'The sickness of democracy', *FP*, p. 178.

16 'The four freedoms: Freedom from fear (continued), *FP*, p. 37.

17 Ibid.

18 For example, one of the few republican flourishes during the constitutional conventions of the 1890s was by New South Wales MP Sir George Dibbs, who described himself 'as one possessing a slight tinge of republican notions, as one who sees that the future of Australia is to be what was prophesied of it fifty years ago, by poets who have written of what the future of Australia is to be—having a certain tinge of republicanism in my nature, the result naturally of my being a descendant of an Englishman' (*Official Report of the National Australasian Convention Debates, Sydney 1891*, George Stephen Chapman, Acting Government Printer, Sydney, 1891, p. 185). Dibbs, who drifted from Presbyterianism to the Church of England, was also a life-long admirer of the Presbyterian minister and republican John Dunmore Lang.

19 Menzies, 'Politics as an art', in *Speech is of Time*, pp. 184–5.

20 Ibid., p. 183.

21 Ibid., pp. 190–1.

22 Ibid., p. 188.

23 'The nature of democracy', *FP*, p. 172.

24 'The four freedoms: Freedom of worship', *FP*, p. 24.

25 See Portus' autobiography, *Happy Highways*, Melbourne University Press, Carlton, 1953. See ch. 6, 'Crisis', for his loss of faith narrative.

26 On Menzies' religion, see D. Furse-Roberts, 'The essential religious belief of Sir Robert Menzies', *Quadrant*, 30 May 2020. See also Roy Williams, *In God They Trust? The Religious Beliefs of Australia's Prime Ministers 1901–2013*, Bible Society Australia, Sydney, 2013, chapter on Menzies.

27 Copy of personal confidential diary for Overseas Journey—19/2/35–8/9/35, Robert Menzies Papers, NLA, MS 4936, Box 572.

28 Ibid., p. 55.

29 Ibid., p. 57.

30 Ibid.

31 Grimley, 'The religion of Englishness', pp. 884–5.

32 R.G. Menzies, *For a Liberal Australia: Essence of the Policy Speech 1949*, The Land Newspaper, Sydney, 1949, p. 3.

33 Copy of personal confidential diary for Overseas Journey—19/2/35–8/9/35, p. 83.

34 Ibid., p. 88.

35 'Menzies to his parents', 18 May 1938, Robert Menzies Papers, NLA, MS 4936, Box 572, Folder: Letters of Menzies to Family 1938–1955.

36 Wolffe, *God and Greater Britain*, p. 262.

37 Green, *The Passing of Protestant England*, p. 118.

38 Copy of personal confidential diary for Overseas Journey—19/2/35–8/9/35, p. 17.

39 The literature is huge, but see Winship, *Godly Republicanism*.

40 Hughes-Warrington & Tregenza, 'State and civilization in Australian new idealism, 1890–1950', pp. 89–108. I. Tregenza, *Journal of Religious History*, vol. 34, no. 3, 2010, pp. 335–53.

41 'The Christian citizen in a new era', speech delivered at St Columba Presbyterian Church, Woollahra, NSW, 11am, Sunday 27 February 1944, p. 1, Robert Menzies Papers, NLA, MS 4936, Box 253, Folder 13.

42 'Democracy and management', First William Queale Memorial Lecture, Adelaide, 22 October 1954, in Menzies, *Speech is of Time*, p. 207.

43 '[T]he theories of life should be woven into the texture of life as it is lived; the abrogation of that time-honoured belief that speculation and execution are mutually exclusive' (Menzies, 'The place of the university in the life of the state', p. 38).

44 Eggleston, *Search for a Social Philosophy*, pp. 327–8.

45 See for example the work of British political philosopher A.D. Lindsay: G. Maddox, 'A.D. Lindsay and modern democratic theory', *Balliol College Annual Record*, 1997, pp. 11–18; cf. Jacques Maritain: '[D]emocracy is linked to Christianity … and … the democratic impulse has arisen in human history as a temporal manifestation of the inspiration of the Gospel' (*Christianity and Democracy*, Geoffrey Bles, London, 1945, pp. 24–5).

46 Menzies, 'Is democracy doomed?', p. 4.

47 Ibid., p. 6.

48 'The ethics of popular self-government [n.d.]', p. 4. Robert Menzies Papers, NLA, MS 4936, Box 251, Folder 2.

49 'Democracy and management', pp. 194–5.

50 Ibid., p. 196.

51 'The sickness of democracy', *FP*, p. 176; cf. 'Democracy and management', p. 196.

52 'The sickness of democracy', *FP*, p. 178.

53 Eggleston, *Search for a Social Philosophy*, p. 324.

54 R.G. Menzies, 'Post-war international relations', in *Post-War Reconstruction in Australia*, Australiasian Publishing with Australian Institute of Political Science, Sydney, 1944, p. 50.

55 Ibid., p. 50.

56 The way Menzies described the university was close to the way Coleridge described the church: 'The object of the National Church, the third remaining estate of the realm, was to secure and improve that civilization, without which the nation could be neither permanent nor progressive' (S.T. Coleridge, *On the*

Constitution of Church and State according to the Idea of Each [1830], J.M. Dent & Sons, London, 1972).

5 EDUCATING FOR SPIRIT

1 A.G. Austin, *Australian Education 1788–1900: Church, State and Public Education in Colonial Australia*, Sir Isaac Pitman & Sons, Melbourne, 1961.

2 See Chavura, Gascoigne & Tregenza, *Reason, Religion and the Australian Polity*, ch. 5.

3 The major secondary sources for Menzies' part in the second education revolution are B. Besant, 'Robert Gordon Menzies and education in Australia', *Melbourne Studies in Education*, vol. 47, nos 1 & 2, 2006, pp. 163–87; A.W. Martin, 'R.G. Menzies and the Murray Committee', in A.W. Martin, *The 'Whig' View of Australian History and Other Essays*, ed. J.R. Nethercote, Melbourne University Press, Melbourne, 2007, pp. 176–205; H. Forsyth, *A History of the Modern Australian University*, NewSouth, Sydney, 2014; G. Harman, in *The Menzies Era: A Reappraisal of Government, Politics and Policy*, ed. S. Prasser, J.R. Nethercote & J. Warhurst, Hale & Iremonger, Sydney, 1995. For Menzies' own account of his education policy, see Menzies, *The Measure of the Years*, pp. 81–97.

4 On Anderson's educational ideas, see also J. Anderson, *Education and Inquiry*, ed. D.Z. Phillips, Blackwell Oxford, 1980. On Anderson's views on liberal education, see G. Melleuish, 'Democracy, utilitarianism and the ideal of liberal education in Australia', *Knowledge Cultures*, vol. 3, no. 3, 2015, pp. 136–40. Our reading of Anderson is also informed by Ian Tregenza's discussion in Chavura, Gascoigne & Tregenza, *Reason, Religion and the Australian Polity*, pp. 213–17.

5   J. Anderson, 'The place of the academic in modern society', in *Education and Inquiry: John Anderson*, ed. Phillips, p. 214. Cited in Chavura, Gascoigne & Tregenza, *Reason, Religion and the Australian Polity*, p. 216.

6   Anderson, 'Socrates and education' (1931), in *Studies in Empirical Philosophy*, p. 206.

7   Anderson, 'Classicism', in *Studies in Empirical Philosophy*, p. 189.

8   On the three competing ideas of a university in Australian history—culture, utility, critique—see S.A. Chavura, 'Culture, utility and critique: The idea of a university in Australia', in *Campus Meltdown: The Deepening Crisis in Australian Universities*, ed. W.O. Coleman, Connor Court, Redland Bay, Qld, 2019, pp. 213–31.

9   Woolley was appointed professor of classics, but he taught widely across the humanities, especially philosophy.

10 J. Woolley, 'Oration at the Inauguration of the University of Sydney, Oct. 11 1852', in *Lectures Delivered in Australia*, Cambridge and London: Macmillan & Co., 1862, pp. 15–16.

11 R.G. Menzies, *The Place of a University in the Modern Community*, Melbourne University Press, Melbourne, 1939, p. 9.

12 Ibid., p. 10.

13 Ibid., p. 12.

14 Ibid., p. 12.

15 In this respect Australia was not alone. The physical destruction of the civilised world released an optimism among many intellectuals that civilisation could be rebuilt *de novo* on the basis of progressive scientific principles. It was the same kind of optimism that inspired utopian treatises that were themselves inspired by the discovery of the Americas.

See K. Lowe, *The Fear and the Freedom: How the Second World War Changed Us*, St Martin's Press, New York, 2017. For Australia in particular, see S. Macintyre, *Australia's Boldest Experiment: War and Reconstruction in the 1940s*, NewSouth, Sydney, 2015.

16 R.G. Menzies, 'Post-war international relations', in *Post-War Reconstruction in Australia*, Australiasian Publishing with Australian Institute of Political Science, Sydney, 1944, p. 15.

17 Ibid., p. 30.

18 Eggleston, *Search for a Social Philosophy*, pp. 320–30.

19 Appointed lecturer in mental and moral philosophy at the University of Queensland in 1911, Mayo went on to have a career at Harvard University. He was one of the most influential and controversial social scientists of his day.

20 The organic metaphor, ubiquitous in the history of social thinking but expressed influentially by St Paul (1 Cor. 12:13–18). See E. Troeltsch, *The Social Teaching of the Christian Churches* [1911], trans. O. Wyon, two vols, Allen & Unwin, London, vol. 1, 1931, pp. 76–7.

21 R.G. Menzies, 'The challenge to education', in R.G. Menzies et al., *The Challenge to Australian Education*, F.W. Cheshire, Melbourne, 1961, p. 5.

22 See G. Melleuish, 'The Machiavellians in our universities', *Quadrant*, February 2018.

23 C. Hazlehurst, *Menzies Observed*, George Allen & Unwin, Sydney, 1979, p. 20.

24 C. Pybus, *Gross Moral Turpitude: The Orr Case Reconsidered*, William Heinemann, Melbourne, 1993; H. Forsyth, 'The Russel Ward case: Academic freedom in Australia during the Cold War', *History Australia*, vol. 11, no. 3, 2014, pp. 31–52.

25 Franklin, *Corrupting the Youth*, pp. 283–6.

26 Horne, *The Lucky Country*, p. 225. Italics added.

27 See also Melleuish, 'The Machiavellians in our universities'.

28 Menzies, *Speech is of Time*, p. 34.

29 'The forgotten people', *FP*, p. 6.

30 Ibid., p. 30.

31 'Speech by the Rt Hon R.G. Menzies, KC MP on education', 30 July 1945, pp. 1415–16, Robert Menzies Papers, NLA, MS 4936, Box 253, Folder 15.

32 R.G. Menzies, 'Australia Today—Man to Man Series—No. 26', Wednesday 17 March 1954, p. 4, Robert Menzies Papers, NLA, MS 4936, Box 257, Folder: Various Broadcasts 1953–54.

33 Menzies, 'The challenge to education', p. 4.

34 Ibid., pp. 11–12.

35 J.R. Darling, *The Education of a Civilized Man*, F.W. Cheshire, Melbourne, 1962, p. 28.

36 'The future of education', broadcast Friday 18 February 1943, Robert Menzies Papers, NLA, MS 4936, Box 253, Folder 13.

37 'Speech by the Hon. R.G. Menzies on Education', Parliamentary Debates, 26 July 1945, p.4615, Robert Menzies Papers, NLA, MS 4936, Box 253, Folder 15.

38 Ibid., p. 4616.

39 Ibid. Cf. 'Politics as an art', *New York Times Magazine*, 28 November 1948, in *Speech is of Time*, p. 187.

40 'Politics as an art', p. 183.

41 'Freedom in modern society' [n.d.; 1935–36?], in *Speech is of Time*, p. 218.

42 Ibid.

43 Ibid., p. 60. On the reception of Hilaire Belloc's writings in Australia, see I. Tregenza, 'The "servile state" Down Under: Hilaire Belloc and Australian political thought, 1912–1953', *Journal of the History of Ideas*, vol. 82, no. 2, 2021.

44 'Speech by the Hon. R.G. Menzies on Education', p. 4616.

45 Ibid., pp. 4616–17.

46 Ibid., p. 4617.

47 Menzies, *The Measure of the Years*, pp. 93–5.

48 R.G. Menzies, 'Australia Today—Man to Man Series—No. 26', Wednesday 17 March 1954, p. 1, Robert Menzies Papers, NLA, MS 4936, Box 257, Folder: Various Broadcasts 1953–54.

49 Ibid., p. 2.

50 Ibid., p. 3.

51 'Freedom in modern society' (no date), in *Speech is of Time*, p. 221.

52 Ibid., p. 223.

53 K. Murray, *Report of the Committee on Australian Universities*, Commonwealth Government Printer, 1957, Canberra.

54 *Australian Universities: Ministerial Statement in Connexion with Report of Committee*, 28 November 1957, Parliament of Australia, p. 4.

55 Ibid., p. 9.

56 Menzies, 'The challenge to education', p. 6.

57 Ibid., p. 7.

58 Ibid., p. 12.

59 'Modern science and civilization', 1958, in *Speech is of Time*, p. 230.

60 Ibid., p. 240.

61 Ibid.

62 Ibid., p. 241.

63 Ibid., p. 245.

64 C. Campbell & G. Sherington, *The Comprehensive High School: Historical Perspectives*, Palgrave Macmillan, New York, 2006, p. 74.

65 J.B. Conant, 'Confidential report to the Carnegie Corporation James B. Conant [*sic*] on the university situation in Australia in the year 1951', *History of Education Review*, vol. 39, no. 1, 2010, pp. 8–22; H. Forsyth, 'Academic work in Australian universities in the 1940s and 1950s', *History of Education Review*, vol. 39, no. 1, 2010, pp. 44–52.

66 P.H. Partridge, 'The Australian universities', in *Taking Stock: Aspects of Mid-Century Life in Australia*, ed. W.V. Aughterson, F.W. Cheshire, Melbourne, 1953, p. 52.

67 This might say something about Australian culture; my great-grandfather left money in his will to the American college that he had attended in the 1880s (GM).

68 Murray, *Report of the Committee on Australian Universities*, p. 24.

69 Besant, 'Robert Gordon Menzies and education in Australia', p. 178.

70 N. Annan, *Our Age: Portrait of a Generation*, Weidenfeld & Nicolson, London, 1990, p. 382.

71 Murray, *Report of the Committee on Australian Universities*, p. 122.

72 Martin, 'R.G. Menzies and the Murray Committee', pp. 198–9.

73 Ibid., p. 203; Hazlehurst, *Menzies Observed*, p. 379.

74 Forsyth, *History of the Modern Australian University*, p. 59.

75 Martin, 'R.G. Menzies and the Murray Committee', p. 203.

76 Sir Robert Menzies, *The Universities—Some Queries*, Wallace Wurth Memorial Lecture, University of NSW, Sydney, 1954, p. 14.

77 Sir Robert Menzies, Official Opening and Dedication at the Senior School Building, Mount Scopus Memorial College, 16 September 1960, pp.12–13, Robert Menzies Papers, NLA, MS 4936, MS 4936, Box 210, Folder 131.

78 On the origins and nature of Australian secular education, see Chavura, Gascoigne & Tregenza, *Reason, Religion and the Australian Polity*, ch. 5.

79 Menzies, 'The challenge to education', p. 2.

CONCLUSION: AUSTRALIAN LIBERALISM AND THE FORGOTTEN MENZIES

1 J.H. Newman, *An Essay in Aid of a Grammar of Assent*, Christian Classics, Westminster, MD, 1973.

2 Menzies, *Central Power in the Australian Commonwealth*, p. 54.

3 Ibid.

4 B. Webb, *Our Partnership*, London, 1948, p. 417, cited in M. Freeden, 'The coming of the welfare state', in *The Cambridge History of Twentieth-century Political Thought*, ed. T. Ball & R. Bellamy, Cambridge University Press, Cambridge, 2003, p. 28.

5 Freeden, 'The coming of the welfare state', p. 28.

6 Calwell, *Be Just and Fear Not*, pp. 243–9.

7 C. Champion, *The Strange Demise of British Canada: The Liberals and Canadian Nationalism, 1964–68*, McGill-Queens University Press, Montreal, 2010.

8 D. Riesman, N. Glazer & R. Denney, *The Lonely Crowd: A Study of the Changing American Character* [1950], Doubleday, New York, Abridged, 1953, pp. 184–5.

9 W.H. Whyte, *The Organization Man*, Penguin, Harmondsworth, 1956, p. 22.

10 E. Lunn, 'Beyond "mass culture": The lonely crowd, the uses of literacy and the post-war era', *Theory and Society*, vol. 19, no. 1, 1990, p. 66; W.F. McClay, 'Fifty years of the lonely crowd', *Wilson Quarterly*, vol. 22, no. 3, 1998, p. 41.

11 M. Harris, 'Morals and manners', in *Australian Civilization*, ed. P. Coleman, Cheshire, Melbourne, 1962, p. 52. In 1961

Hugh Gough, Anglican Archbishop of Sydney, criticised the pernicious influence of John Anderson on sexual morality in Australia. Gough saw a new spirit in Australia 'decrying the institution of marriage [and] advocating free love and right of self-expression' (Anon., *Free Spirit: Bulletin of the Australian Association for Cultural Freedom*, vol. 7, no. 3/4, 1961, p. 1).

12 See for example M. Lilla, *The Once and Future Liberal: After Identity Politics*, Harper, New York, 2017. For the Australian context, see Chavura, Gascoigne & Tregenza, *Reason, Religion and the Australian Polity*, ch. 11.

13 Z. Gorman & G. Melleuish, 'The nexus clause: A peculiarly Australian obstacle', *Cogent Arts and Humanities*, vol. 5, no. 1, 2018.

14 It was mirroring similar trends around the world. See H. McLeod, *The Religious Crisis of the 1960s*, Oxford University Press, Oxford, 2010. On secularisation in Australia, see D. Hilliard, 'Australia: Towards secularisation and one step back', in *Secularisation in the Christian World: Essays in Honour of Hugh McLeod*, ed. C. Brown & M. Snape, Routledge, Abingdon, 2016, pp. 76–90; D. Hilliard, 'The religious crisis of the 1960s: The experience of the Australian churches', *Journal of Religious History*, vol. 21, no. 2, 1997, pp. 209–27.

15 See M. Arrow, *The Seventies: The Personal, the Political and the Making of Modern Australia*, NewSouth, Sydney, 2019. Quotes from the report are from Chavura, Gascoigne & Tregenza, *Reason, Religion and the Australian Polity*, p. 237.

16 On vocational and economic shifts in Australia, see J. Carroll, *Land of the Golden Cities: Australia's Exceptional Prosperity and the Culture That Made It*, Connor Court, Redland Bay, Qld, 2017.

17 M. Lopez, *The Origin of Multiculturalism in Australian Politics: 1945–1975*, Melbourne University Press, Carlton, 2000.

18 Green, *The Passing of Protestant England*, p. 34.

19 Ibid., p. 35.

20 As embodied in T.H. Marshall's influential essay, *Citizenship and Social Class: And Other Essays*, Cambridge University Press, Cambridge, 1950. See Tregenza, 'From virtues to values'.

21 Having said this, the rise of 'wokeness', or the popularisation of postmodern and cultural Marxist/critical theory discourses around sexuality and race, with their preoccupation with identity politics, is making the Whitlamesque Left also appear at best quaint, at worst oppressive.

22 Cultural critics could speak of 'a puritanical, insular, monotonous country like Australia' (D. McCallum, 'The state of liberty', in Coleman, *Australian Civilization*, pp. 29; cf. pp. 34, 39, 59).

23 In 1948 Menzies could privately admit: 'It is no doubt quite true, unhappily, that Great Britain by herself is no longer a first rate power.' See R.G. Menzies to D. Bradman, 9 March 1948, p. 2, Robert Menzies Papers, NLA, MS 4936, Box 5, Folder 34).

24 For Menzies' pessimism about the future of Australia, see R.G. Menzies to [Lady] Violet Braddon, 12 November 1974, Robert Menzies Papers, NLA, MS 4936, Box 5, Folder 34.

BIBLIOGRAPHY

ARCHIVAL SOURCES

Charles Henry Pearson Papers, State Library of Victoria, Box 436/1, MS57153

John Latham Papers, National Library of Australia, MS 1009, Box 45

Patrick McMahon Glynn Papers, National Library of Australia, MS 4653, Box 1, Series 3

Robert Menzies Papers, National Library of Australia, MS 4936 (many boxes)

OFFICIAL GOVERNMENT DOCUMENTS

Australian Universities: Ministerial Statement in Connexion with Report of Committee, 28 November 1957, Parliament of Australia

Official Report of the National Australasian Convention Debates (Third Session): Melbourne 1898, Robert S. Brain, Government Printer, Melbourne, 1898

Official Report of the National Australasian Convention Debates, Sydney 1891, George Stephen Chapman, Acting Government Printer, Sydney, 1891

Official Record of the Proceedings and Debates of the Australasian Federation Conference, 1890, Robert S. Brain, Government Printer, Victoria, 1890

GENERAL SOURCES

Aladdin, 'Science and mind', *Melbourne University Magazine*, vol. 10, no. 3, 1916, p. 90

Anderson, J., *Education and Inquiry*, ed. D.Z. Phillips, Blackwell Oxford, 1980

—— *Studies in Empirical Philosophy*, Angus & Robertson, Sydney, 1962

Annan, N., *Our Age: Portrait of a Generation*, Weidenfeld & Nicolson, London, 1990

Anon., *Free Spirit: Bulletin of the Australian Association for Cultural Freedom*, vol. 7, no. 3/4, 1961

Arrow, M., *The Seventies: The Personal, the Political and the Making of Modern Australia*, NewSouth, Sydney, 2019

Austin, A.G., *Australian Education 1788–1900: Church, State and Public Education in Colonial Australia*, Sir Isaac Pitman & Sons, Melbourne, 1961

Baker, D.W.A., *Days of Wrath: A Life of John Dunmore Lang*, Melbourne University Press, Carlton, 1985

Belich, J., *Replenishing the Earth: The Settler Revolution and the Rise of the Anglo World, 1783–1939*, Oxford University Press, Oxford, 2009

Benson, S., 'Battle to claim the Menzies legacy a shot across the bow', *Australian*, 11 July 2017, www.theaustralian.com.au/opinion/battle-to-claim-the-menzies-legacy-a-shot-across-the-bow/news-story/130e813349d53ff538f053e0401a5b3d

Berg, C., 'Adam Smith and Jeremy Bentham in the Australian colonies', *History of Economics Review*, vol. 68, no. 1, 2017, pp. 2–16

Besant, B., 'Robert Gordon Menzies and education in Australia', *Melbourne Studies in Education*, vol. 47, nos 1 & 2, 2006, pp. 163–87

Brett, J., *Australian Liberals and the Moral Middle Class: From Alfred Deakin to John Howard*, Cambridge University Press, Cambridge, 2003

—— *The Enigmatic Mr Deakin*, Text Publishing, Melbourne, 2017

—— *Robert Menzies' Forgotten People*, Melbourne University Press, Carlton, 2nd edn, 2007

Calwell, A.A., *Be Just and Fear Not*, Lloyd O'Neil, Melbourne, 1972

Campbell, C. & G. Sherington, *The Comprehensive High School: Historical Perspectives*, Palgrave Macmillan, New York, 2006

Carr, A. & B.T. Jones, 'Civic republicanism and Sir Robert Menzies: The non-liberal side of the Liberal leader', *Journal of Australian Studies*, vol. 37, no. 4, 2013, pp. 485–502

Carroll, J., *Land of the Golden Cities: Australia's Exceptional Prosperity and the Culture That Made It*, Connor Court, Redland Bay, Qld, 2017

Champion, C., *The Strange Demise of British Canada: The Liberals and Canadian Nationalism, 1964–68*, McGill-Queens University Press, Montreal, 2010

Chavura, S.A., 'Culture, utility and critique: The idea of a university in Australia', in *Campus Meltdown: The Deepening Crisis in Australian Universities*, ed. W.O. Coleman, Connor Court, Redland Bay, Qld, 2019, pp. 213–31

Chavura, S.A., J. Gascoigne & I. Tregenza, *Reason, Religion and the Australian Polity: A Secular State?* Routledge, London, 2019

Chavura, S.A. & G. Melleuish, 'Conservative instinct in Australian political thought: The Federation debates, 1890–1898', *Australian Journal of Political Science*, vol. 50, no. 3, pp. 513–28

Chifley, B., 'For freedom,' in *Justice Now! Social Justice Statements of the Australian Catholic Bishops 1940–1966*, ed. M. Hogan, Department of Government and Public Administration, University of Sydney, Sydney, 1990, pp. 26–37

—— 'Petrol rationing—An unpopular duty', in *Things Worth Fighting For: Speeches by Joseph Benedict Chifley*, ed. A.W. Stargardt, Melbourne University Press, Melbourne, 1952

Coleman, P. (ed.), *Australian Civilization*, F.W. Cheshire, Melbourne, 1962

Coleridge, S.T., *On the Constitution of Church and State according to the Idea of Each* [1830], J.M. Dent & Sons, London, 1972

Colley, L., *Britons: Forging the Nation: 1707–1837* [1992], Yale University Press, New Haven and London, 2nd edn, 2005

Collins, H., 'Political ideology in Australia: The distinctiveness of a Benthamite society', in *The Daedalus Symposium*, ed. S.R. Graubard, Angus & Robertson, Sydney, 1985, pp. 147–69

Conant, J.B., 'Confidential report to the Carnegie Corporation James B. Conant [*sic*] on the university situation in Australia in the year 1951', *History of Education Review*, vol. 39, no. 1, 2010, pp. 8–22

Darling, J.R., *The Education of a Civilized Man*, F.W. Cheshire, Melbourne, 1962

Davidson, J., *A Three-cornered Life: The Historian W.K. Hancock*, UNSW Press, Sydney, 2010

Deakin, A., *The Federal Story: The Inner History of the Federal Cause*, Robertson & Mullens, Melbourne, 1944. http://adc.library.usyd.edu.au/data-2/fed0002.pdf

De Sanctis, A., *The 'Puritan' Democracy of Thomas Hill Green*, Imprint Academic, Exeter, 2005

Eggleston, F., *Search for a Social Philosophy*, Melbourne University Press, Melbourne, 1941

Ely, R.G., 'The religion of John West: Orthodox Protestant, deist, atheist, or what?', *Lucas: An Evangelical History Review*, nos 25 & 26, 1999, pp. 46–74

Forsyth, H., 'Academic work in Australian universities in the 1940s and 1950s', *History of Education Review*, vol. 39, no. 1, 2010, pp. 44–52

—— *A History of the Modern Australian University*, NewSouth, Sydney, 2014

—— 'The Russel Ward case: Academic freedom in Australia during the Cold War', *History Australia*, vol. 11, no. 3, 2014, pp. 31–52

Franklin, J., *Corrupting the Youth: A History of Philosophy in Australia*, Macleay Press, Sydney, 2003

Freeden, M., 'The coming of the welfare state', in *The Cambridge History of Twentieth-Century Political Thought*, ed. T. Ball & R. Bellamy, Cambridge University Press, Cambridge, 2003, pp. 7–44

Freeman, D., *Abbott's Right: The Conservative Tradition from Menzies to Abbott*, Melbourne University Press, Carlton, 2017

Furse-Roberts, D., 'The essential religious belief of Sir Robert Menzies', *Quadrant*, 30 May 2020. https://quadrant.org.au/magazine/2020/06/the-essential-religious-belief-of-robert-menzies/

Gibbs, D.R., 'Victorian school books: A study of the changing social content and use of school books in Victoria, 1848–1948, with particular reference to school readers', PhD thesis, University of Melbourne, 1987

Gorman, Z., & G.C. Melleuish, 'The nexus clause: A peculiarly Australian obstacle', *Cogent Arts and Humanities*, vol. 5, no. 1, 2018. https://ro.uow.edu.au/cgi/viewcontent.cgi?article=4660&context=lhapapers

Green, S.J.D., *The Passing of Protestant England: Secularisation and Social Change c. 1920–1960*, Cambridge University Press, Cambridge, 2011

Green, T.H., *Lectures on the Principles of Political Obligation and Other Writings*, ed. P. Harris & J. Morrow, Cambridge University Press, Cambridge, 1986

Grimley, M., 'The religion of Englishness: Puritanism, providentialism and "national character", 1918–1945', *Journal of British Studies*, vol. 46, no. 4, 2007, pp. 884–906

Hancock, W.K., *Argument of Empire*, Penguin, Harmondsworth, 1943

—— *Australia* [1930], Ernest Benn, London, 1945

—— 'Classics', *Melbourne University Magazine*, vol. XI, no. 2, 1917, pp. 49–51

Harman, G., 'Development of higher education', in *The Menzies Era: A Reappraisal of Government, Politics and Policy*, ed. S. Prasser, J.R. Nethercote & J. Warhurst, Hale & Iremonger, Sydney, 1995

Harris, M., 'Morals and manners', in *Australian Civilization*, ed. P. Coleman, Cheshire, Melbourne, 1962, pp. 47–67

Hazlehurst, C., *Menzies Observed*, George Allen & Unwin, Sydney, 1979

Hearn, M., 'A transnational imagination: Alfred Deakin's reading lists', in *Transnational Ties: Australian Lives in the World*, ed. D. Deacon, P. Russell & A. Woollacott, ANU E-Press, Canberra, 2008

Hilliard, D., 'Australia: Towards secularisation and one step back', in *Secularisation in the Christian World: Essays in Honour of Hugh McLeod*, ed. C. Brown & M. Snape, Routledge, Abingdon, 2016, pp. 76–90

—— 'The religious crisis of the 1960s: The experience of the Australian churches', *Journal of Religious History*, vol. 21, no. 2, 1997, pp. 209–27

Hirst, J., *The Strange Birth of Colonial Democracy: New South Wales 1848–1884*, Allen & Unwin, North Sydney, 1988

Hodgson, M.G.S., *Rethinking World History: Essays on Europe, Islam and World History*, Cambridge University Press, Cambridge, 1993

Horne, D., *The Lucky Country: Australia in the Sixties* [1964], Penguin, Harmondsworth, 2nd edn, 1968

Hudson, W., *Australian Religious Thought*, Monash University Press, Clayton, 2016

Hughes, W.M., *Crusts and Crusades*, Angus & Robertson, Sydney, 1948

Hughes-Warrington, M. & I. Tregenza, 'State and civilization in Australian new idealism, 1890–1950', *History of Political Thought*, vol. 29, no. 1, 2008, pp. 89–108

Jones, H., *Idealism as a Practical Creed*, James Maclehose & Sons, Glasgow, 1909

Keating, P., 'Gough broke "Menzian torpor": Keating', *SBS News*, 21 October 2014. www.sbs.com.au/news/gough-broke-menzian-torpor-keating

Kemp, D., *The Land of Dreams: How Australians Won their Freedom 1788–1860*, Miegunyah Press, Carlton, 2018

—— 'Liberalism, conservatism and the growth of government in Australia', in *Liberalism and Conservatism*, ed. G. Melleuish, Connor Court, Ballarat, 2015

La Nauze, J.A. & Nurser, E. (eds), *Walter Murdoch and Alfred Deakin on Books and Men: Letters and Comments 1900–1918*, Melbourne University Press, Melbourne, 1974

Lilla, M., *The Once and Future Liberal: After Identity Politics*, Harper, New York, 2017

Lopez, M., *The Origin of Multiculturalism in Australian Politics: 1945–1975*, Melbourne University Press, Carlton, 2000

Lowe, K., *The Fear and the Freedom: How the Second World War Changed Us*, St Martin's Press, New York, 2017

Lunn, E., 'Beyond "mass culture": The lonely crowd, the uses of literacy and the post-war era', *Theory and Society*, vol. 19, no. 1, 1990, pp. 63–86

McCallum, D., 'The state of liberty', in *Australian Civilization*, ed. P. Coleman, F.W. Cheshire, Melbourne, 1962, pp. 26–46

Macintyre, S., *Australia's Boldest Experiment: War and Reconstruction in the 1940s*, NewSouth, Sydney, 2015

—— *A Colonial Liberalism: The Lost World of Three Victorian Visionaries*, Oxford University Press, Melbourne, 1991

McClay, W.F., 'Fifty years of the lonely crowd', *Wilson Quarterly*, vol. 22, no. 3, 1998, pp. 34–42

McLeod, H., *The Religious Crisis of the 1960s*, Oxford University Press, Oxford, 2010

Maddox, G., 'A.D. Lindsay and modern democratic theory', *Balliol College Annual Record*, 1997, pp. 11–18

—— *Religion and the Rise of Democracy*, Routledge, London, 1996

Malouf, D., 'Australia's British inheritance', in *Four Classic Quarterly Essays on the Australian Story*, Black Inc., Melbourne, 2006

Maritain, J., *Christianity and Democracy*, Geoffrey Bles, London, 1945

Marshall, T.H., *Citizenship and Social Class: And Other Essays*, Cambridge University Press, Cambridge, 1950

Martin, A.W., 'Faction, politics and the education question in New South Wales', in *Melbourne Studies in Education, 1960–61*, ed. E.L. French, Melbourne University Press, Melbourne, 1962, pp. 25–47

—— *Henry Parkes: A Biography*, Melbourne University Press, Carlton, 1980

—— 'R.G. Menzies and the Murray Committee', in A.W. Martin, *The 'Whig' View of Australian History and Other Essays*, ed. J.R. Nethercote, Melbourne University Press, Melbourne, 2007, pp. 176–205

Melleuish, G., 'Democracy, utilitarianism and the ideal of liberal education in Australia', *Knowledge Cultures*, vol. 3, no. 3, 2015, pp. 136–40

—— *Despotic State or Free Individual: Two Traditions of Democracy in Australia*, Australian Scholarly Press, Melbourne, 2014

—— 'The Machiavellians in our universities', *Quadrant*, February 2018. https://quadrant.org.au/magazine/2018/01-02/machiavellian-takeover-australian-universities/

—— 'The theology and philosophy of John Woolley', *Journal of Religious History*, vol. 12, no. 4, 1983, pp. 418–32

—— 'E.G. Whitlam: Reclaiming the initiative in Australian history', in *Making Modern Australia: The Whitlam Government's 21st Century Agenda*, ed. J. Hocking, Monash University Press, Clayton, 2017, pp. 308–35

Melleuish, G. (ed.), *Liberalism and Conservatism*, Connor Court, Ballarat, 2015

Melleuish, G. & S.A. Chavura, 'Utilitarianism contra sectarianism: The official and the unauthorized civic religion of Australia', in *Only in Australia: The History, Politics and Economics of Australian Exceptionalism*, ed. W. Coleman, Oxford University Press, Oxford, 2016, pp. 62–80

Menzies, R.G., *Afternoon Light: Some Memories of Men and Events*, Cassell, Melbourne, 1967

—— *Central Power in the Australian Commonwealth*, Cassell, London, 1967

—— 'The challenge to education', in R.G. Menzies et al., *The Challenge to Australian Education*, F.W. Cheshire, Melbourne, 1961

—— 'Education and truth', *Melbourne University Magazine*, vol. X, no. 1, 1916, p. 4

—— *For a Liberal Australia: Essence of the Policy Speech 1949*, The Land Newspaper, Sydney, 1949

—— *The Changing Commonwealth*, Cambridge University Press, Cambridge, 1960

—— *The Forgotten People and Other Studies in Democracy*, Angus & Robertson, Sydney, 1943

—— *The Measure of the Years*, Cassell, London, 1970

—— *The Place of a University in the Modern Community*, Melbourne University Press, Melbourne, 1939

—— 'Post-war international relations', in *Post-War Reconstruction in Australia*, Australasian Publishing with Australian Institute of Political Science, Sydney, 1944, pp. 11–66

—— *Speech is of Time: Selected Speeches and Writings*, Cassell, London, 1958

—— *'To the People of Britain at War': From the Prime Minister of Australia. Speeches by the Right Honourable Robert Gordon Menzies delivered in Great Britain in 1941*, Longmans, Green & Co., London, 1941

—— 'The place of the university in the life of the state', *Melbourne University Review*, vol. X, no. 2, 1916, pp. 37–8

—— *The Universities—Some Queries*, Wallace Wurth Memorial Lecture, University of New South Wales, Sydney, 1954

—— 'What are we fighting for?', *Melbourne University Magazine*, vol. 10, no. 3, 1916, p. 74

More, T., *Utopia* [1516], trans. P. Turner, Penguin, Harmondsworth, 1965

Murdoch, W., *The Australian Citizen: An Elementary Account of Civic Rights and Duties*, Whitcombe & Tombs, Melbourne, 1912

—— *Alfred Deakin* [1923], Bookman Press, Melbourne, 1999

Murphy, J., *Evatt: A Life*, NewSouth, Sydney, 2016

Murray, K., *Report of the Committee on Australian Universities*, Commonwealth Government Printer, 1957, Canberra

Newman, J.H., *Apologia Pro Vita Sua: Being a History of His Religious Opinions*, Oxford University Press, London, 1964

—— *An Essay in Aid of a Grammar of Assent*, Christian Classics, Westminster, MD, 1973

Parkes, H., *The Electoral Act and How to Work It: A Series of Letters on the Subject of the Approaching Elections*, Sydney, 1859

—— *Mr Gladstone and English Liberalism from an Australian Point of View*, Lee & Ross, Sydney, 1878

Partridge, P.H., 'The Australian universities', in *Taking Stock: Aspects of Mid-century Life in Australia*, ed. W.V. Aughterson, F.W. Cheshire, Melbourne, 1953

Penton, B., *Think or Be Damned: A Subversive Note on National Pride, Patriotism and Other Forms of Ostrichism Practised in Australia*, Angus & Robertson, Sydney, 1941

Piggin, S. & R.D. Linder, *The Fountain of Public Prosperity: Evangelical Christians in Australian History 1740–1914*, Monash University Publishing, Clayton, 2018

Portus, G.V., *Happy Highways*, Melbourne University Press, Carlton, 1953

Pybus, C., *Gross Moral Turpitude: The Orr Case Reconsidered*, William Heinemann, Melbourne, 1993

Rickard, J., *H.B. Higgins: The Rebel as Judge*, Allen & Unwin, Sydney, 1984

Riesman, D., N. Glazer & R. Denney, *The Lonely Crowd: A Study of the Changing American Character* [1950], Doubleday, New York, Abridged, 1953

Robinson, H.G.R., *Speeches Delivered by His Excellency Sir Hercules G.R. Robinson*, Gibbs, Shallard & Company, Sydney, 1879

Roe, J., *Beyond Belief: Theosophy in Australia 1879–1939*, UNSW Press, Sydney, 1986

Royce, J., *The Philosophy of Josiah Royce*, ed. J.K. Roth, Thomas Y. Crowell Co., New York, 1971

Samuel, R., 'The discovery of puritanism, 1820–1914: A preliminary sketch', in *Revival and Religion since 1700: Essays for John Walsh*, ed. J. Garnett & C. Matthew, Bloomsbury Academic, London, 1993, pp. 201–47

Santayana, G., *The Philosophy of Santayana*, ed. I. Edman, Modern Library, New York, 1936

Sawer, M., *The Ethical State? Social Liberalism in Australia*, Melbourne University Press, Carlton, 2003

Scott, S., 'Chisholm, Alan Rowland (1888–1981)', *Australian Dictionary of Biography*, National Centre of Biography, Australian National University, 2007. http://adb.anu.edu.au/biography/chisholm-alan-rowland-12315/text22121

Shann, E., *Bond or Free? Occasional Economic Essays*, Angus & Robertson, Sydney, 1930

Siedentop, L., *Inventing the Individual: The Origins of Western Liberalism*, Harvard University Press, Cambridge, MA, 2014

'Smawnsh', 'Have we any culture?', *Melbourne University Magazine*, vol. X, no. 1, 1916

Smith, A.G., 'Laurie, Henry (1837–1922)', *Australian Dictionary of Biography*, National Centre of Biography, Australian National University, 1986. http://adb.anu.edu.au/biography/laurie-henry-7106/text12255

Smuts, J.C., *Holism and Evolution*, Macmillan, London, 1927

Todd, M., *Christian Humanism and Puritan Social Order*, Cambridge University Press, Cambridge, 1987

Tregenza, I., 'From virtues to values: Conceptions of Australian citizenship', in *From Migrant to Citizen: Testing Language, Testing Culture*, ed. C. Slade & M. Möllering, Palgrave Macmillan, London, 2010, pp. 60–76

—— 'The idealist tradition in Australian religious thought', *Journal of Religious History*, vol. 34, no. 3, 2010, pp. 335–53

—— 'The "servile state" Down Under: Hilaire Belloc and Australian political thought, 1912–1953', *Journal of the History of Ideas*, vol. 82, no. 2, 2021

Trevelyan, G.M., *English Social History: A Survey of Six Centuries, Chaucer to Queen Victoria*, Longmans, Green & Co., London, 1942

Troeltsch, E., *The Social Teaching of the Christian Churches* [1911], trans. O. Wyon, two vols, Allen & Unwin, London, vol. 1, 1931

Tucker, T.G., *Platform Monologues*, Thomas C. Lothian, Melbourne, 1914

Van Onselen, P., 'Liberal Party reactionaries ignore Menzies' progressive vision', *Australian*, 17 February 2017, www.theaustralian.com.au/opinion/columnists/peter-van-onselen/liberal-party-reactionaries-ignore-menzies-progressive-vision/news-story/2985dc52e769a89e0a7413ac07411e3b

Waldron, J., *God, Locke and Equality: Christian Foundations in Locke's Political Thought*, Cambridge University Press, Cambridge, 2002

West, J., *Union among the Colonies*, ed. G. Melleuish, Australian Scholarly Publishing, Kew, Vic, 2001

Whyte, W.H., *The Organization Man*, Penguin, Harmondsworth, 1956

Williams, Raymond, *Culture and Society 1780–1950* [1958], Pelican, London, 1971

Williams, Roy, *In God They Trust? The Religious Beliefs of Australia's Prime Ministers 1901–2013*, Bible Society Australia, Sydney, 2013

Wilson, A.N., *God's Funeral*, Abacus, London, 1999

Winship, M.P., *Godly Republicanism: Puritans, Pilgrims and a City on a Hill*, Harvard University Press, Cambridge, MA, 2012

Wolffe, J., *God and Greater Britain: Religion and National Life in Britain and Northern Ireland 1843–1945*, Routledge, London, 1994

Woolley, J., *Inaugural Address [delivered in] Maitland, on the opening of [the School of Arts]*, Robert Wisdom and the *Northern Times*, Maitland, NSW, 1857

——— 'Oration at the Inauguration of the University of Sydney, Oct. 11 1852', in *Lectures Delivered in Australia*, Cambridge and London: Macmillan & Co., 1862, pp. 15–16

INDEX